GRADE
6

patterns

graphs

graphs

charts

FLASH
FORWARD
TEST PREP

spelling

context

Written by **Christy Yaros**

Illustrations by **Ed Shems**

Cover illustration by Hector Borlasca
Cover design by Loira Walsh
Interior design by Gladys Lai
Edited by Eliza Berkowitz

Flash Kids
A Division of Barnes & Noble
122 Fifth Ave
New York, NY 10011

ISBN: 978-1-4114-1620-8

Please submit all inquiries to FlashKids@bn.com

Printed and bound in the United States

1 3 5 7 9 10 8 6 4 2

Dear Parent,

Test taking can be challenging for kids. In the face of test questions, answer bubbles, and the ticking clock, it's easy to see why tests can be overwhelming. That's why it's vital that children prepare for tests beforehand. Knowing the material is only part of preparing for tests. It's equally important that children practice answering different types of questions, filling in answers, and pacing themselves through test material. Children who practice taking tests develop confidence and can relax during the real test.

This Flash Forward Test Prep book will give your child the opportunity to practice taking tests in reading and math. Each practice test is based on national standards, so you know your child is reviewing important material he or she should be learning in the sixth grade. In addition to reinforcing sixth-grade curriculum, this book allows your child to practice answering different kinds of test questions. Best of all, each unit ends with a four-page practice test that reviews all the material in that unit. This truly gives kids a chance to show what they know and to see their progress.

The more practice children have before taking a test, the more relaxed and confident they will be during the exam. As your child works through the book, he or she will start to develop test-taking strategies. These strategies can be utilized during a real test. By the time your child finishes the book, he or she will be ready to tackle any exam, from the annual standardized test to the weekly pop quiz!

Table of Contents

Section 7: Statistics, Data Analysis, and Probability

Section 8: Mathematical Reasoning

Test-Taking Tips

Preparing for a test starts with your mind and body. Here are some things you can do before the test to make sure you're ready.

- A few days before the test, get together with friends from your class to review the material. Have fun quizzing each other.

- The night before the test, go to bed early and get plenty of sleep.

- Eat a healthy breakfast the morning of the test.

- Find out beforehand if you need a pencil, eraser, or pen, and make sure you pack them in your schoolbag.

- Before you leave for school, do a few practice test questions at home to get warmed up.

- Remember to use the restroom before the test begins.

- Have confidence in yourself. A positive attitude will help you do well!

Once the test has started, you need to stay focused. Here are some tips to keep in mind during the test.

- Always begin by reading or listening carefully to the directions.

- Make sure you read all the answer choices before choosing the one you think is correct.

- If you get stuck on a certain question, it's okay to skip it. Go back to the question later.

- Work at your own pace. Don't pay attention to how quickly other students are completing the test.

- Fill in the answer bubbles completely and neatly.

- If you finish the test before time is up, use the time to review your answers.

- Take time to double check any questions you felt uncertain about. Make sure you want to stick with your answer.

Here are some tips to keep in mind when taking reading and language tests.

- Read each question or passage slowly and carefully.

- Say words in your head and think about the sounds.

- Underline important words in the question that tell you what you need to do.

- As you read a passage, underline key words and phrases.

- Use context clues to help figure out the meaning of a word you might not know.

- Cross out answers you know are wrong. Then focus on the remaining choices.

- It's okay to go back to the passage or sentence and reread it.

These tips will help you as you work on math tests.

- Find out if you can use a piece of scratch paper or part of the test booklet to work through math problems.

- Make sure you understand each question before you choose an answer. Reread the question if you need to.

- Solve a problem twice and make sure you get the same answer both times.

- Try plugging in the answer choices to see which one makes a true math sentence.

- When you're solving word problems or story problems, underline key words that tell you what to do.

- Draw a picture to help you visualize the right answer.

- Pay attention to the operation signs and make sure you know if you need to add, subtract, multiply, or divide.

Section 1: Reading

Main Idea and Supporting Details

Read the passages and answer the questions.

Discovering Electricity

You probably believe that Benjamin Franklin discovered electricity in 1752 when his kite was struck by lightning. However, electricity had already been discovered by this time. Instead, Franklin was looking to prove that lightning was electricity.

Franklin did indeed fly a silk kite with a metal key near the end of the string during a storm. He noticed that the fibers on the string stood up, as if they were charged. He touched the key and felt a charge—but it was from the built-up electricity in the air, not a lightning strike. With this, he was able to prove his theory.

If Franklin's kite really had been struck by lightning, he probably would have died. Professor Georg Wilhelm Richmann of St. Petersburg, Russia, suffered this fate when he tried the same experiment shortly after Franklin.

1. What is the main idea of this passage?
   - Ⓐ Benjamin Franklin discovered electricity.
   - Ⓑ Georg Wilhelm Richmann discovered electricity.
   - Ⓒ Franklin's kite experiment was trying to prove that lightning was electricity.
   - Ⓓ You can make electricity in a thunderstorm with a kite and a key.

2. What made the fibers on the string stand up?
   - Ⓐ the key
   - Ⓑ a lightning strike
   - Ⓒ electricity from the kite
   - Ⓓ electricity in the air

3. What proved Franklin's theory?
   - Ⓐ The kite string burned up from the lightning.
   - Ⓑ The kite was struck by lightning and the key got hot.
   - Ⓒ He felt a charge when he touched the key.
   - Ⓓ The kite still flew even though there was a storm.

4. Which transition word tells you that the first sentence is being disproved?
   - Ⓐ However
   - Ⓑ If
   - Ⓒ Indeed
   - Ⓓ Already

Blackbeard, the Famous Pirate

Maybe you've heard of the famous pirate Blackbeard and his mysterious treasure. Blackbeard earned a frightening reputation. His reign of terror focused on the West Indies and the Atlantic coast of North America. His headquarters were in North Carolina and the Bahamas.

You see, the Spanish would get gold and silver from Mexico and South America and send their treasure on ships back to Spain. Blackbeard and his crew would then attack these ships and steal the treasure for themselves. Although he spent only about two years on the high seas, he accumulated a large amount of wealth. His end came in November 1718, when a British lieutenant decapitated the pirate and hung his head as a trophy.

Still, no one knows what happened to Blackbeard's vast treasure. He acknowledged burying it, but its location was never disclosed. Countless treasure hunters have been trying to get their hands on it ever since. Blackbeard's sunken ship, *Queen Anne's Revenge*, was supposedly discovered near Beaufort, North Carolina, in 1996. No loot was onboard. The mystery of Blackbeard's treasure continues to intrigue nearly 300 years after it was lost.

5. What is this passage mostly about?
  Ⓐ North Carolina and the Bahamas
  Ⓑ the Spanish and their treasure
  Ⓒ how to search for buried treasure
  Ⓓ Blackbeard and his lost treasure

6. How did Blackbeard get his treasure?
  Ⓐ He got it from Mexico.
  Ⓑ He got it from the Spanish.
  Ⓒ He got it from South America.
  Ⓓ He got it from North Carolina.

7. What information is known about the treasure?
  Ⓐ It sunk with *Queen Anne's Revenge*.
  Ⓑ It was buried in Mexico.
  Ⓒ It was buried somewhere unknown.
  Ⓓ The Spanish got it all back.

8. Where was Blackbeard's sunken ship found?
  Ⓐ the Bahamas
  Ⓑ North Carolina
  Ⓒ Spain
  Ⓓ Mexico

Understanding Real-Life Materials

Read the two pieces of information below. Use them to answer the questions.

Watertown Little League Baseball Sign-Ups	
Who is eligible[1]: Residents of Watertown	
Divisions:	
Pony (ages 13–14)	Pinto (ages 7–8)
Bronco (ages 11–12)	Shetland "A" (ages 5–6)
Mustang (ages 9–10)	Shetland "B" (ages 4–5)
[1]For verification of age and residency you must bring an original birth certificate and THREE documents, such as one utility bill, one school record, driver's license, and homeowner or tenant record.	
Tryouts:	
Pinto—January 12	Pony—January 19
Mustang—January 13	Shetland Evaluations—January 20
Bronco—January 19	

REGISTRATIONS WILL NOT BE ACCEPTED AFTER TRYOUTS

Early Bird Registration Fee $75.00 ($85.00 after Thursday, January 10)
Uniform Fee: $35.00   Trophy Fee: $10.00

WATERTOWN LITTLE LEAGUE PLAYER REGISTRATION FORM	League use only Date received:

Player Name: _____
Address: _____
Address 2: _____
City/State/Zip: _____
E-mail: _____

League: _____
Birthdate: _____
Gender: _____
Home Phone: _____
Lives with: ___Mother ___Father ___Both

Parent #1
Name: _____ Phone #1: _____
E-mail: _____ Phone #2: _____

Parent #2
Name: _____ Phone #1: _____
E-mail: _____ Phone #2: _____

Medical Information

Emergency Contact: _____
(Can be a parent)
Relationship to Player: _____

Phone: _____
Insurance Carrier: _____
Policy Number: _____

CONSENT FOR MEDICAL TREATMENT
I, AS THE PARENT OR LEGAL GUARDIAN OF THE ABOVE NAMED PLAYER, HEREBY GIVE MY CONSENT FOR EMERGENCY MEDICAL CARE ADMINISTERED BY A DULY LICENSED PHYSICIAN, DENTIST, HOSPITAL, CLINIC, OR PARAMEDIC. THIS CARE MAY BE GIVEN UNDER WHATEVER CONDITIONS ARE NECESSARY TO PRESERVE LIFE, LIMB, OR WELL-BEING OF MY DEPENDENT.

Signature: _____   Date: _____

1. What division should Matt sign up for if he is 11 years old?
   - (A) Pony
   - (B) Bronco
   - (C) Mustang
   - (D) Pinto

2. When are Mustang tryouts?
   - (A) January 12
   - (B) January 13
   - (C) January 19
   - (D) January 20

3. When would a 14-year-old try out?
   - (A) January 12
   - (B) January 13
   - (C) January 19
   - (D) January 20

4. Which two leagues hold tryouts on the same day?
   - (A) Pinto and Mustang
   - (B) Pinto and Bronco
   - (C) Bronco and Pony
   - (D) Pony and Shetland

5. What is **not** an example of the type of document needed to verify age and residency?
   - (A) social security card
   - (B) original birth certificate
   - (C) utility bill
   - (D) school record

6. How much is registration on January 8?
   - (A) $75.00
   - (B) $35.00
   - (C) $10.00
   - (D) $85.00

7. Which of the following would **not** count as something to verify your residency?
   - (A) utility bill
   - (B) homeowner record
   - (C) magazine subscription
   - (D) driver's license

8. Which information on the registration form is for league use only?
   - (A) Player Name
   - (B) Home Phone
   - (C) E-mail
   - (D) Date received

9. Who signs the "Consent for Medical Treatment" section?
   - (A) the player
   - (B) the coach
   - (C) a doctor
   - (D) a parent

10. Which piece of information is **not** required on the form?
    - (A) birthdate
    - (B) grade
    - (C) league
    - (D) zip code

Analyzing Real-Life Materials

Look at the bus schedule and fare information below. Use it to answer the questions.

Plainville	Caston		Rivertown		Deerfield		Westfield
Departure	Arrival	Departure	Arrival	Departure	Arrival	Departure	Arrival
7:10	**7:17**	**7:19**	**8:37**	**8:47**	**9:05**	**9:07**	**9:43**
7:35			**→ 8:45**	**8:55**			**→ 9:47**
9:00	**9:07**	**9:09**	10:27	10:37	10:55	10:57	11:33
1:05	1:12	1:14	2:32	2:42	3:00	3:02	3:38
4:10	4:17	4:19	5:37	5:47	6:05	6:08	6:52
5:05	5:12	5:14	6:32	6:42	7:00	7:02	7:39
5:30			→ 6:40	6:50			→ 7:35
6:05	6:12	6:14	7:32	7:42	8:00	8:02	8:38
8:05	8:12	8:14	9:32	9:42	10:00	10:02	10:38
10:05	10:12	10:14	11:32	11:42	12:00	12:02	12:38

→ denotes express   Times in bold are AM

Transit Fares				
			Off-Peak Hours	Peak Hours
Adults (Ages 13–64)		Local Fare (per stop)	$1.50	$2.00
		Express Fare (per stop)	$2.00	$2.75
Seniors (65+), **Youth** (6–12) & **Medicare card holders**		Local Fare (per stop)	$0.50	$2.00
		Express Fare (per stop)	$0.50	$2.75
Person with disabilites		Any Trip (per stop)	$0.50	$0.50
Peak Hours: Monday–Friday 6:00-9:00 AM and 3:00–6:30 PM				

1. When does the first bus leave Plainville for Westfield?
   Ⓐ 6:05
   Ⓑ 7:10
   Ⓒ 4:10
   Ⓓ 8:05

2. If you leave Plainville at 1:05 PM, what time will you arrive in Deerfield?
   Ⓐ 2:32 AM
   Ⓑ 2:42 PM
   Ⓒ 3:00 AM
   Ⓓ 3:00 PM

3. You live in Plainville and are going to meet your cousin for lunch in Westfield. You have to be there by 11:45 AM. What time does the last bus that you can take leave Plainville?
   Ⓐ 7:35 AM
   Ⓑ 8:45 AM
   Ⓒ 9:00 AM
   Ⓓ 10:37 AM

4. You are traveling from Rivertown to Deerfield but cannot leave before 7:30 PM. What is the earliest time you can arrive in Deerfield?
   Ⓐ 7:42 PM
   Ⓑ 8:00 PM
   Ⓒ 10:00 PM
   Ⓓ 10:38 PM

5. What is the second stop if you leave Plainville at 5:30?
   Ⓐ Caston
   Ⓑ Rivertown
   Ⓒ Deerfield
   Ⓓ Westfield

6. Of all the buses that leave Plainville, which one arrives in Westfield in the shortest amount of time?
   Ⓐ 5:30 PM
   Ⓑ 4:10 PM
   Ⓒ 9:00 AM
   Ⓓ 7:35 AM

7. How much would an 11-year-old have to pay to go from Plainville to Caston on the 1:05 bus?
   Ⓐ $1.50
   Ⓑ $2.00
   Ⓒ $0.50
   Ⓓ $2.75

8. How much would a senior pay to go from Plainville to Westfield on the 5:30 bus?
   Ⓐ $0.50
   Ⓑ $1.00
   Ⓒ $4.00
   Ⓓ $5.50

9. How much does a local fare for a child cost per stop off-peak?
   Ⓐ $1.50
   Ⓑ $2.00
   Ⓒ $0.50
   Ⓓ $2.75

10. Which of the following buses from Plainville is off-peak?
    Ⓐ 7:10
    Ⓑ 9:00
    Ⓒ 6:05
    Ⓓ 8:05

Understanding Persuasive Texts

Read the passage and answer the questions.

Build a Skate Park, Help a Community

Skateboarding and in-line skating are popular pastimes with the youth of today. Unfortunately, there is no safe place in Huntington for skaters. Twin Forks Park has a rarely used basketball court that should be turned into a skate park.

With nowhere to go, skateboarders are forced to skate in streets and parking lots, where they create dangers for pedestrians and cars. Street skating causes damage to public and private property. This irritates business owners and increases police involvement.

Skaters are going to skate, regardless of local laws or the attitudes of business owners. Skateboarding is an athletic activity that requires skill, just like baseball or football. It should be given the same importance when it comes to providing facilities. Statistics show that skateboarding results in fewer injuries than organized sports, including baseball and basketball. It is the perfect sport for those who just want to get away from the TV and do something active without the pressures of organized sports.

Communities can come together at skate parks. Instead of the eight to ten people at a time who can enjoy the basketball courts, skate parks allow for dozens of people to join in—as skaters or spectators. Skate parks can be built to fit any budget or area.

A skate park will also bring increased revenue to the town. Since there are no other skate parks in the area, parents will bring their children to Huntington. While they are here, they will likely spend their money at our local shops and restaurants.

People say that skateboarders are bad. They think kids congregating can lead to vandalism and increased garbage, but that's not true. A skate park is an easy way to give Huntington's children a safe environment. Kids can have fun, spend time with friends, and steer clear of things like drugs that could get them in trouble.

1. What could the author have included in paragraph 3 to strengthen the argument that skateboarding "results in fewer injuries" than organized sports?
   Ⓐ a newspaper story on the dangers of organized sports
   Ⓑ a quotation from a basketball player about injuries he's had
   Ⓒ a chart comparing injuries from skateboarding and organized sports
   Ⓓ a statement from a school nurse about treating injuries

2. Which of the following sources would provide the **best** evidence to support the last statement in paragraph 4?
   Ⓐ pictures of people enjoying skate parks
   Ⓑ a magazine about the history of skateboarding
   Ⓒ a story about a famous skateboarder
   Ⓓ a book of different layouts and prices of skate parks

3. Choose a sentence that would strengthen the argument below.
   > People say that skateboarders are bad. They think kids congregating can lead to vandalism and increased garbage, but that's not true.
   Ⓐ After all, a centralized place would make it easier for police to patrol.
   Ⓑ After all, not all kids like to vandalize and litter.
   Ⓒ After all, kids will be too busy skateboarding to vandalize.
   Ⓓ After all, kids could still vandalize the basketball court.

4. Which sentence from the article is an unsupported opinion?
   Ⓐ Communities can come together at skate parks.
   Ⓑ Street skating causes damage to public and private property.
   Ⓒ It is the perfect sport for those who just want to get away from the TV and do something active without the pressures of organized sports.
   Ⓓ Unfortunately, there is no safe place in Huntington for skaters.

5. Why did the author write this article?
   Ⓐ to persuade the town to get rid of the basketball courts
   Ⓑ to persuade the town to build a skate park for kids
   Ⓒ to inform people about the joys of skateboarding
   Ⓓ to inform people of the dangers of organized sports

6. Which sentence from the passage is a generalization?
   Ⓐ While they are here, they are likely to spend their money at our local shops and restaurants.
   Ⓑ People say that skateboarders are bad.
   Ⓒ Street skating causes damage to public and private property.
   Ⓓ Statistics show that skateboarding results in fewer injuries than organized sports including baseball and basketball.

Finding Facts

Read the passage and answer the questions.

Coins

When you hear coins jingling in your pocket, do you wonder about the history of coins as currency? The first coins were minted, or produced, in Lydia, an ancient empire located in modern-day Turkey. Around 640 BCE, King Croesus began making small pieces of metal stamped with an imperial emblem.

The Greeks followed this trend, and later the Romans. Usually made of gold or silver, the value of the coins was determined by the issuing government. For example, if Spartan officials stated all coins minted in Sparta were 87 percent gold, then the coin's worth would be based on the value of gold.

About the same time as they were developed in the West, coins appeared in China. The Chinese began using a form of money around the fifth century BCE. Shaped like knives or tools, there was a round hole at one end so the money could be strung onto a rope or rod. They became smaller and smaller over the years, until they were only a rounded part with a hole in it. These coins hardly changed until the 1800s.

An important effect of coins was that governments could control both the release of money into the market and the money supply. Roman emperors would reduce the amount of gold and silver in Roman coins when they needed money. They thought that, if a ton of silver made 5,000 silver coins, they could cut the silver content in half and have twice as many coins. Constantly making coins worth less led to an unstable economy, however. This led to the eventual collapse of the Roman Empire.

When Rome fell, most of Europe became distrustful of coins. Coins as currency fell out of use. In the Renaissance, however, coins made a comeback. Today in the United States, we use coins all the time, though they are no longer made of gold.

1. Who were the first people to use coins?
   Ⓐ Romans
   Ⓑ Greeks
   Ⓒ Lydians
   Ⓓ Chinese

2. What was Chinese money first shaped like?
   Ⓐ knives
   Ⓑ ropes
   Ⓒ rods
   Ⓓ ingots

3. What were coins usually made from?
   Ⓐ gold and knives
   Ⓑ gold and silver
   Ⓒ silver and tools
   Ⓓ knives and tools

4. What did Roman emperors do when they needed money?
   Ⓐ They made more coins.
   Ⓑ They took coins from Greece.
   Ⓒ They used less silver in their coins.
   Ⓓ They made coins smaller.

5. Who made coins with holes in them?
   Ⓐ Romans
   Ⓑ Greeks
   Ⓒ Lydians
   Ⓓ Chinese

6. When did coins stop being used?
   Ⓐ during the Renaissance
   Ⓑ after Rome fell
   Ⓒ in 640 BCE
   Ⓓ in the fifth century BCE

7. Where was Lydia located?
   Ⓐ in China
   Ⓑ in Rome
   Ⓒ in Sparta
   Ⓓ in Turkey

8. Who decided how much a coin was worth?
   Ⓐ King Croesus
   Ⓑ Sparta
   Ⓒ the issuing government
   Ⓓ the emperor

9. What happened to coins during the Renaissance?
   Ⓐ They were used to control the supply of gold.
   Ⓑ They became highly collectible.
   Ⓒ They fell out of favor.
   Ⓓ They became popular again.

10. What are coins today **not** made from?
   Ⓐ copper
   Ⓑ zinc
   Ⓒ gold
   Ⓓ nickel

Understanding Informational Texts

Read the passage and answer the questions.

Will You Turn that Down?

Have you ever come home from a long day at school, put on your headphones, and kicked back to your favorite songs on your MP3 player? It may help you relax, but prolonged exposure to noise can harm your hearing.

We experience sound in our environment daily, from television, radio, household appliances, and traffic. Usually these sounds are at safe levels. However, exposure to sounds that are too loud or last a long time can be harmful. Small sensory cells in our inner ear, called hair cells, can be damaged, resulting in noise-induced hearing loss (NIHL). Once damaged, hair cells cannot grow back.

Both one-time exposures to intense "impulse" sounds, like an explosion, and constant long-term exposure to loud sounds, like in a factory, can cause NIHL. Sound loudness is measured in units called decibels. For example, normal conversation is around 60 decibels. Loud noises, like firecrackers and rock concerts, emit sounds between 110 and 150 decibels. Long or repeated exposure to sounds at or above 85 decibels can cause hearing loss.

Although you should definitely be aware of decibel levels, distance from the source of the sound and duration of exposure to the sound are equally important. You should avoid noises that are "too loud" and "too close" or last "too long." You can prevent NIHL from both impulse and continuous noise by regularly using hearing protectors such as earplugs or earmuffs.

As for that MP3 player, a good rule of thumb is that the music is too loud if you can't hear someone nearby talking. At maximum volume, you can cause hearing loss in just 8 to 15 minutes! However, if you keep those tunes at 50 percent volume, you can safely rock out to your heart's content.

1. Why did the author write this passage?
- Ⓐ to persuade readers to buy an MP3 player
- Ⓑ to inform about the dangers of loud noises
- Ⓒ to entertain with a humorous story
- Ⓓ to convince readers not to lose their hearing

2. At what decibel level does the risk of hearing loss begin?
- Ⓐ 60 decibels
- Ⓑ 85 decibels
- Ⓒ 110 decibels
- Ⓓ 150 decibels

3. Which of the following types of noises should you **not** avoid?
- Ⓐ too loud
- Ⓑ too close
- Ⓒ too long
- Ⓓ too soft

4. What gets damaged causing hearing loss?
- Ⓐ hair cells
- Ⓑ hair follicles
- Ⓒ inner ear
- Ⓓ outer ear

5. Which of these is the **best** summary of the passage?
- Ⓐ You should avoid all noises at all costs.
- Ⓑ If you're going to listen to music, make it loud.
- Ⓒ There are many different sounds in the world.
- Ⓓ Being smart about noise levels can save your hearing.

6. What does the author mean by "to your heart's content" in the last paragraph?
- Ⓐ a little bit
- Ⓑ until your heart is happy
- Ⓒ as much as you want
- Ⓓ to fill up your heart

Look at the chart below. Use it to answer questions 7–8.

How loud is too loud?		
150	Firecracker	
120	Ambulance siren	
110	Chainsaw, Rock concert	**110 Decibels** Regular exposure to more than 1 minute risks permanent hearing loss.
105	MP3 player at maximum level	
100	Wood shop, Snowmobile	**100 Decibels** No more than 15 minutes unprotected exposure recommended.
95	Motorcycle	
90	Power mower	
85	Heavy city traffic	**85 Decibels** Prolonged exposure to any noise above 85 decibels can cause gradual hearing loss.
60	Normal conversation	
40	Refrigerator humming	
30	Whispered voice	

7. Which of these can cause hearing loss if exposed to for too long?
- Ⓐ whispered voice
- Ⓑ a normal conversation
- Ⓒ a refrigerator humming
- Ⓓ a motorcycle

8. How long can you listen to a snowmobile before you risk damage?
- Ⓐ indefinitely
- Ⓑ 15 minutes
- Ⓒ 1 minute
- Ⓓ 30 seconds

Narrative Analysis

Read the story and answer the questions.

Whitewashing the Fence

Tom appeared on the sidewalk with a bucket of whitewash and a brush. He surveyed the fence. He began to think of the fun he had planned for this day, and his sorrows multiplied. At this dark and hopeless moment an inspiration burst upon him!

Ben ranged up alongside of him and said, "Hello, I'm going swimming. Don't you wish you could? You'd rather WORK—wouldn't you? Course you would!"

Tom answered carelessly: "All I know is, it suits Tom Sawyer."

"Oh come, now, you don't mean to let on that you LIKE it?"

The brush continued to move.

"Like it? Does a boy get a chance to whitewash a fence every day?"

That put the thing in a new light. Tom swept his brush back and forth, Ben watching every move and getting more interested. He said, "Say, Tom, let ME whitewash a little." Tom considered, was about to consent; but he altered his mind. "No, Aunt Polly's awful particular about this fence. I reckon there ain't one boy in a thousand, maybe two thousand, that can do it the way it's got to be done."

"Lemme try. Say—I'll give you the core of my apple. I'll give you ALL of it!"

Tom gave up the brush with reluctance in his face, but eagerness in his heart. He planned the slaughter of more innocents. Boys happened along and remained to whitewash. Tom had traded the next chance to Billy Fisher for a kite; Johnny Miller bought in for a dead rat and a string to swing it with. And when the middle of the afternoon came, Tom was literally rolling in wealth. He had twelve marbles, a piece of blue bottle-glass to look through, a spool cannon, a key, a fragment of chalk, a glass stopper of a decanter, a tin soldier, a couple of tadpoles, six fire crackers, a kitten with only one eye, a brass doorknob, a dog-collar, the handle of a knife, four pieces of orange-peel, and an old window sash.

The fence had three coats of whitewash on it! If he hadn't run out of whitewash he would have bankrupted every boy in the village.

—adapted from *The Adventures of Tom Sawyer* by Mark Twain

1. What is Tom's mood in the beginning of the story?
   Ⓐ sad
   Ⓑ happy
   Ⓒ excited
   Ⓓ bored

2. What word **best** describes Tom?
   Ⓐ simple
   Ⓑ clever
   Ⓒ mean
   Ⓓ caring

3. How does Tom trick the boys into giving him things?
   Ⓐ He offers them an apple.
   Ⓑ He pretends that painting is fun.
   Ⓒ He won't let them paint the fence.
   Ⓓ He offers them whatever they want.

4. What is Tom's main problem in the beginning of the story?
   Ⓐ His friends are trying to trick him.
   Ⓑ He wants to paint the fence, but Ben won't let him.
   Ⓒ He doesn't want to spend all day painting.
   Ⓓ The village boys keep bothering him.

5. At the end of the story, why does Tom have such a large pile of treasure?
   Ⓐ Aunt Polly gave him gifts for painting the fence.
   Ⓑ He wanted to give treasures to his friends for helping him.
   Ⓒ He traded his own treasures to his friends.
   Ⓓ He tricked many boys into painting the fence for him.

6. Read the sentences below. Why does Ben say this to Tom?
   "Hello, I'm going swimming. Don't you wish you could? You'd rather WORK —wouldn't you? Course you would!"
   Ⓐ Ben wants Tom to come with him.
   Ⓑ Ben does not like to go swimming.
   Ⓒ Ben wants to make Tom jealous.
   Ⓓ Ben likes to ask a lot of questions.

7. Where does this story mostly take place?
   Ⓐ at the fence
   Ⓑ at the swimming hole
   Ⓒ at Ben's house
   Ⓓ in Aunt Polly's house

8. Why did the author write this story?
   Ⓐ to persuade people to learn to paint
   Ⓑ to entertain with a funny story
   Ⓒ to warn people about being tricked
   Ⓓ to teach how to whitewash a fence

9. What probably would have happened if Tom didn't come up with a plan to trick the boys?
   Ⓐ Aunt Polly would have finished painting the fence.
   Ⓑ Tom would have gone swimming with Ben.
   Ⓒ The boys would have helped him paint anyway.
   Ⓓ Tom would have spent all day painting by himself.

10. How does Tom begin to solve his problem?
    Ⓐ He asks Aunt Polly to let him go swimming.
    Ⓑ He paints the fence as fast as he can.
    Ⓒ He tricks Ben into helping him paint.
    Ⓓ He pays the neighborhood boys to paint.

Understanding Poetry

Read the poem and answer the questions.

Romance
by Gabriel Setoun

1 I saw a ship a-sailing,
2 A-sailing on the sea;
3 Her masts were of the shining gold,
4 Her deck of ivory;
5 And sails of silk, as soft as milk,
6 And silver shrouds had she.

7 And round about her sailing,
8 The sea was sparkling white,
9 The waves all clapped their hands and sang
10 To see so fair a sight.
11 They kissed her twice, they kissed her thrice,
12 And murmured with delight.

13 Then came the gallant captain,
14 And stood upon the deck;
15 In velvet coat, and ruffles white,
16 Without a spot or speck;
17 And diamond rings, and triple strings
18 Of pearls around his neck.

19 And four-and-twenty sailors
20 Were round him bowing low;
21 On every jacket three times three
22 Gold buttons in a row;
23 And cutlasses down to their knees;
24 They made a goodly show.

25 And then the ship went sailing,
26 A-sailing o'er the sea;
27 She dived beyond the setting sun,
28 But never back came she,
29 For she found the lands of the golden sands,
30 Where the pearls and diamonds be.

1. What is this poem mostly about?
    Ⓐ the powerful sea
    Ⓑ sailors' clothing
    Ⓒ an impressive ship
    Ⓓ a fearsome sea captain

2. Read the lines below. What are they an example of?
    9 *The waves all clapped their hands and sang*
    10 *To see so fair a sight.*
    Ⓐ simile
    Ⓑ metaphor
    Ⓒ symbolism
    Ⓓ personification

3. What does the poet compare the sails to?
    Ⓐ pearls
    Ⓑ milk
    Ⓒ diamonds
    Ⓓ ivory

4. What do "she" and "her" refer to in the poem?
    Ⓐ the ship
    Ⓑ the captain
    Ⓒ the sea
    Ⓓ a sailor

5. What is the rhyme scheme of the first stanza?
    Ⓐ A-B-A-B-A-B
    Ⓑ A-B-C-A-B-C
    Ⓒ A-B-C-B-D-B
    Ⓓ A-A-B-B-C-D

6. How do the sailors feel about the captain?
    Ⓐ They don't like him.
    Ⓑ They are afraid of him.
    Ⓒ They respect him.
    Ⓓ They look down at him.

7. Why did the author describe the sea as "sparkling white"?
    Ⓐ because it was white
    Ⓑ to give a clearer image
    Ⓒ to make the poem rhyme
    Ⓓ because it matched the sails

8. How does the author organize this poem?
    Ⓐ in paragraphs
    Ⓑ in chronological order
    Ⓒ in order of importance
    Ⓓ in stanzas

9. From whose point of view is this poem told?
    Ⓐ an observer
    Ⓑ the sea
    Ⓒ the ship
    Ⓓ the crew

10. What does the author use "gold," "ivory," and "silver" to describe?
    Ⓐ the ship
    Ⓑ the sea
    Ⓒ the captain
    Ⓓ the sailors

Using Context Clues

Fill in the missing words in the passage below. Choose the word that sounds best in each sentence.

Opened in 1825, New York's Erie Canal was the engineering __(1)__ of the nineteenth century. When the planning for what many __(2)__ as "Clinton's Folly" began, there was not a single school of engineering in the United States. With the __(3)__ of a few places where black powder was used to blast through mountains, all 363 miles were built by men and horses.

The Erie Canal proved to be the key that unlocked __(4)__ social and economic changes in our young nation. The canal __(5)__ the first great westward movement of American settlers, gave access to the rich land and __(6)__ west of the Appalachians, and made New York the greatest __(7)__ city in the United States.

At the start of the 1800s, the Allegheny Mountains were the western frontier. The Northwest Territories were rich in timber, minerals, and fertile land for farming. It took weeks to reach these __(8)__ resources. Travelers were forced to take __(9)__ turnpike roads that got hard in the summer. In the winter, the roads __(10)__ into a sea of mud.

Then, New York Governor DeWitt Clinton __(11)__ a better way: a canal from Buffalo to Albany. The canal had an immediate and __(12)__ effect as settlers poured west. Within 15 years of the canal's opening, New York was the busiest port in America, moving greater shipments than Boston, Baltimore, and New Orleans combined.

1. (A) disappointment
   (B) marvel
   (C) letdown
   (D) project

2. (A) mocked
   (B) yelled
   (C) laughed
   (D) called

3. (A) inclusion
   (B) addition
   (C) exception
   (D) conception

4. (A) sparse
   (B) numerous
   (C) dangerous
   (D) horrible

5. (A) hindered
   (B) stalled
   (C) injured
   (D) spurred

6. (A) resources
   (B) people
   (C) recourses
   (D) land

7. (A) rural
   (B) communal
   (C) commercial
   (D) inland

8. (A) worthless
   (B) valuable
   (C) valiant
   (D) hidden

9. (A) ancient
   (B) mushy
   (C) smooth
   (D) rutted

10. (A) hardened
    (B) dissolved
    (C) dismissed
    (D) gathered

11. (A) envisioned
    (B) denied
    (C) discouraged
    (D) enveloped

12. (A) unimpressive
    (B) boring
    (C) unfortunate
    (D) dramatic

Section 2: Written and Oral Language Conventions

Forms of Writing

Different kinds of writing require different formats. It is important to know which type of writing to use in a particular situation. Read each question below and choose the correct answer.

1. Paula's town is considering tearing down the only playground to make a parking lot for local businesses. Paula wants people to be aware of what could happen and urge them to help stop it. What should she write?
- Ⓐ a factual report
- Ⓑ a letter to the editor
- Ⓒ a short story
- Ⓓ a narrative poem

2. Jamal is learning about poetry in his English class. His aunt loves poetry. If Jamal wants to write to his aunt to tell her about what he is learning, what should he write?
- Ⓐ a business letter
- Ⓑ a letter of request
- Ⓒ a letter to the editor
- Ⓓ a personal letter

3. Rafael's teacher has asked the class to pretend that they live in another country. They are instructed to conduct research, then write about what they discover. Rafael chooses China as his country. What will Rafael write?
- Ⓐ a book review
- Ⓑ a letter to the editor
- Ⓒ a factual report
- Ⓓ a lyrical poem

4. Li just read a fabulous novel. She thinks it's something that everyone at school should read. She wants to put something in the school newspaper about the book. What should she write?
- Ⓐ a research report
- Ⓑ a book review
- Ⓒ a persuasive essay
- Ⓓ a letter of request

5. Frank's grandparents are celebrating their 50th wedding anniversary. He wants to write something to read at the party that expresses his feelings about them and the values they have given him. What should Frank write?
- Ⓐ a narrative poem
- Ⓑ a research report
- Ⓒ a short story
- Ⓓ a persuasive essay

6. Janene's class has just read a novel about two boys on a quest to find their father. In the end, they find him but he doesn't want to be part of their lives. Her teacher has asked the class to imagine a different ending for the novel. Janene has decided that in her version, the boys will find their father and he will be happy to see them. What will Janene write?
- Ⓐ a persuasive essay
- Ⓑ a personal letter
- Ⓒ a book review
- Ⓓ a short story

7. Tino ordered a model rocket from a website. When he finally received it in the mail, there were broken pieces in the box. He called customer service, but they told him they are not responsible for items damaged in the mail. This made Tino upset. He wants to write a letter to the company. What should he write?
Ⓐ a letter to the editor
Ⓑ a letter of request
Ⓒ a letter of complaint
Ⓓ a friendly letter

8. Darla's teacher has asked the class if they think soda and candy should be sold in the cafeteria. They are to form an opinion and conduct research to back it up. The completed assignments will be passed on to the principal for consideration. What should Darla write?
Ⓐ a persuasive essay
Ⓑ a business letter
Ⓒ a narrative poem
Ⓓ a letter to the editor

9. Kenny's class has just finished reading a story about a dog that saves a family from a potentially devastating fire while they slept. Kenny's teacher has asked the class to write about a pet they have or once had. What should Kenny write?
Ⓐ a personal letter
Ⓑ a persuasive essay
Ⓒ a personal narrative
Ⓓ a narrative poem

10. Jess is writing a report about the tools that ancient civilizations used. If she wants to obtain information from the Museum of Natural History in her city, what should she write?
Ⓐ a personal letter
Ⓑ a letter to the editor
Ⓒ a letter of complaint
Ⓓ a letter of request

11. What is writing that contains stanzas and lines, and may or may not rhyme?
Ⓐ a poem
Ⓑ an essay
Ⓒ a report
Ⓓ a letter

12. What is writing that is based on research, gives information about a specific topic, and has an introduction, supporting paragraphs, and a conclusion?
Ⓐ a report
Ⓑ a poem
Ⓒ an essay
Ⓓ a letter

13. What is writing that tells about the writer's personal experience, is usually written in the first-person point of view, and has a beginning, middle, and an end?
Ⓐ a short story
Ⓑ a narrative
Ⓒ a report
Ⓓ a letter

14. What is writing that gives an opinion about an issue, gives facts to back up the opinion, and has an introductory paragraph, supporting paragraphs, and a conclusion?
Ⓐ a letter to the editor
Ⓑ a factual report
Ⓒ a narrative essay
Ⓓ a persuasive essay

Prewriting and Composing

Takei's favorite cereal is Oaty O's. The company that makes it, Grainworks, has decided not to make it anymore. Takei wants to write a letter to the president of the company and ask him to reconsider. Read the information about letter writing below. Then answer the questions.

1. What kind of letter should Takei write?
Ⓐ a letter to the editor
Ⓑ a business letter
Ⓒ a personal letter
Ⓓ a letter of request

2. If the president of the company's name is Peter Munson, how should Takei address the letter?
Ⓐ Dear Pete,
Ⓑ To whom it may concern:
Ⓒ Dear Mr. Munson:
Ⓓ Mr. Munson,

Takei used this graphic organizer to help him organize his thoughts.
Use it to answer questions 3 and 4.

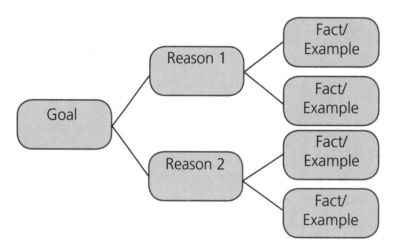

3. What should Takei put under "Goal"?
Ⓐ write a letter
Ⓑ save Oaty O's
Ⓒ have a bowl of Oaty O's
Ⓓ meet the president

4. Which of the following would **not** be good to put under "Reason"?
Ⓐ They taste really good.
Ⓑ They are the most nutritious cereal.
Ⓒ A lot of kids enjoy eating them.
Ⓓ My brother doesn't like them.

5. What is a good opening sentence for Takei's letter?
Ⓐ How are you?
Ⓑ Don't do it.
Ⓒ I am writing to you about Oaty O's.
Ⓓ You better keep making Oaty O's!

6. What is a good closing for Takei to use?
Ⓐ Love always,
Ⓑ Your friend,
Ⓒ Hugs and kisses,
Ⓓ Sincerely,

Tasha is writing an essay about natural energy and material resources.

7. Which of these would **best** help Tasha plan her essay?
- Ⓐ thinking of things that are natural
- Ⓑ asking the teacher for a narrower topic
- Ⓒ asking her parents for help in writing the essay
- Ⓓ making a list of the kinds of natural resources

8. What would be a good topic sentence for Tasha to start her essay?
- Ⓐ There are many things in this world that are natural.
- Ⓑ Resources can be for energy or materials.
- Ⓒ Earth has many natural energy and material resources.
- Ⓓ Wood is a natural resource that can be both energy and material.

9. How should Tasha organize her essay?
- Ⓐ by the categories "renewable" and "nonrenewable"
- Ⓑ in alphabetical order from A to Z
- Ⓒ from least important to most important resource
- Ⓓ by comparing and contrasting energy and material resources

Tasha made this outline to help her write her essay. Use it to answer questions 10–12.

I. Introduction to Natural Resources	Wind
	Trees/Forests
II. Nonrenewable Resources	IV. Conserving Resources
Coal	Why Conserve?
Natural Gas	Ways to Conserve
Minerals	Use Nonrenewable Resources
III. Renewable Resources	Recycle
Solar	V.

10. Where should Tasha put "oil" in her outline?
- Ⓐ II
- Ⓑ III
- Ⓒ IV
- Ⓓ V

11. Which of the following is incorrect on Tasha's outline?
- Ⓐ Coal
- Ⓑ Trees/Forests
- Ⓒ Use Nonrenewable Resources
- Ⓓ Recycle

12. What should go in *V* on Tasha's outline?
- Ⓐ Introduction
- Ⓑ Conclusion
- Ⓒ Ways to Use Resources
- Ⓓ Unnatural Resources

Research and Technology

Paravi is writing a research report about the different dynasties in China. She is in the library doing research. Read about Paravi's research. Then answer the questions.

1. Paravi is trying to look up a book called *Ancient China* in the library's computerized card catalog. This is the screen that comes up:

To look for a book by the author's last name:		To look for a book by title:	
STEP	ACTION	STEP	ACTION
1	Type: FA	1	Type: FT
2	Type: Author's last name	2	Type: Book title
3	Press: <Enter> key	3	Press: <Enter> key

What is the first thing Paravi should type?
Ⓐ FA
Ⓑ FT
Ⓒ Ancient China
Ⓓ <Enter>

2. Paravi found the book called *Ancient China*. In what part of the book would she **most likely** find the titles of other books about the Chinese dynasties?
Ⓐ the copyright page
Ⓑ the bibliography
Ⓒ the glossary
Ⓓ the table of contents

3. What topic should Paravi look for in an encyclopedia to find out more about the Qin Dynasty's unification of northern China?
Ⓐ dynasty
Ⓑ unification
Ⓒ northern
Ⓓ China

4. What would be the **best** key words for an Internet search if Paravi wanted more information about the silk trade in China during the Han Dynasty?
Ⓐ silk trade Han Dynasty
Ⓑ silk China
Ⓒ trade China
Ⓓ Han Dynasty

5. Where is the **best** place for Paravi to find more information about the Great Wall of China's boundaries?
Ⓐ a book about walls
Ⓑ a magazine about travel
Ⓒ a dictionary
Ⓓ an atlas

6. Paravi found a library book about philosophy. Where should she look to see if the book has information about Confucius?
Ⓐ the title page
Ⓑ the index
Ⓒ the glossary
Ⓓ the copyright page

Use the dictionary entry to answer questions 7 and 8.

rul·er (rōō′lər) *n.* 1. a person who rules or governs; sovereign 2. a straight edged strip, as of wood or metal, for drawing straight lines and measuring lengths; also called *rule* 3. a person or thing that rules paper, wood, etc. 4. *Astrology.* the planet primarily associated with any sign of the zodiac or any house of the horoscope: *The ruler of Aries is Mars. The ruler of Taurus is Venus.*

7. In her first draft, Paravi wrote the sentence below. Which definition of *ruler* **best** fits the way Paravi used it in her sentence?

> *"The leader of the Qin declared himself First Emperor and began the tradition of having emperors as rulers."*

Ⓐ 1
Ⓑ 2
Ⓒ 3
Ⓓ 4

8. How would Paravi divide the word *rulers* at the end of a line?
Ⓐ ru-lers
Ⓑ r-ulers
Ⓒ rul-ers
Ⓓ rule-rs

Use the table of contents from the book *Ancient China: The Empire* to answer questions 9 and 10.

9. In which chapter should Paravi look to find information on the teachings of Confucius?
Ⓐ 3
Ⓑ 4
Ⓒ 5
Ⓓ 6

10. On which page should Paravi start looking for information about what inventions came out of Ancient China?
Ⓐ 10
Ⓑ 30
Ⓒ 70
Ⓓ 84

Evaluating and Revising

Read this rough draft of a student's essay. Then answer the questions.

(1) Plate tectonics is a theory to explain changes in the earth's crust caused by forces from within the earth. (2) It was developed in the 1960s and 1970s, when new information was found out about the ocean floor and the worldwide distribution of fossils and rock types.

(3) In 1911, a German meteorologist noticed that Africa and South America seemed to fit together like a jigsaw puzzle. (4) He suggested that Africa and South America had been joined together at one time. (5) They broke apart and drifted to where they are now. (6) The people of Africa and South America speak different languages and have different cultures.

(7) Evidence to support this idea of the continental drift continued to be found. (8) Geologists in Africa and South America found certain structures that ended abruptly at the edge of the continents. (9) When the continents were fitted together on a map, the structures matched up.

(10) The Lystrosaurus was a small reptile that lived a long time ago. (11) Bones from this animal were found in Africa and South America, while teeth were found in Antarctica.

(12) Scientists now state that the earth's outermost layer is broken into seven pieces, called plates. (13) These include the African, North American, South American, Eurasian, Australian, Antarctic, and Pacific plates. (14) There are also several minor plates, including the Arabian, Nazca, and Philippines plates.

(15) The plates are in constant motion, though they move in different directions and at different speeds. (16) Sometimes they crash into each other, which causes earthquakes to occur and mountains and volcanoes to form. (17) Sometimes they pull apart, which explains the continental drift.

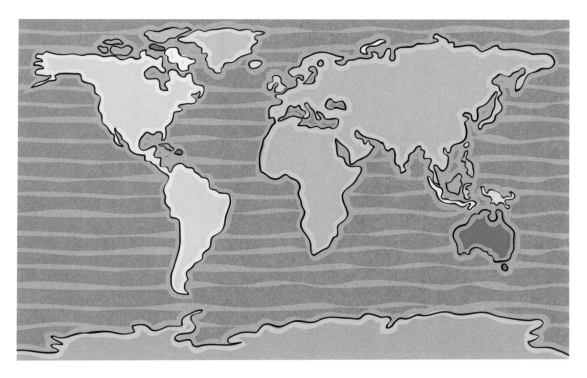

1. Read the two sentences from paragraph 2 below. Which word should be added to the beginning of the second sentence?

> He suggested that Africa and South America had been joined together at one time. They broke apart and drifted to where they are now.

(A) And,
(B) Therefore,
(C) Nonetheless,
(D) Then,

2. Which sentence would be **best** to remove from the essay?

(A) Plate tectonics is a theory to explain changes in the earth's crust caused by forces from within the earth.
(B) The people of Africa and South America speak different languages and have different cultures.
(C) Scientists now state that the earth's outermost layer is broken into seven pieces, called plates.
(D) The plates are in constant motion, though they move in different directions and at different speeds.

3. Which of the following revisions would make sentence 10 more informative?

(A) The Lystrosaurus, a small hippopotamus-like reptile, lived about 200 million years ago.
(B) The Lystrosaurus was a small reptile and it lived about 200 million years ago.
(C) The Lystrosaurus lived about 200 million years ago.
(D) The Lystrosaurus was a small hippopotamus-like reptile.

4. Read the sentence below. For which paragraph in the rough draft would this be the **best** introductory sentence?

> Biological evidence also supported the idea.

(A) the first paragraph
(B) the second paragraph
(C) the third paragraph
(D) the fourth paragraph

5. Read the two sentences from paragraph 3 below. Which word should be added to the beginning of the second sentence?

> Geologists in Africa and South America found certain structures that ended abruptly at the edge of the continents. When the continents were fitted together on a map, the structures matched up.

(A) Since,
(B) However,
(C) Nonetheless,
(D) Because,

6. Which of these sentences would be **best** to add as the last sentence of the fourth paragraph?

(A) When earthquakes do happen, they cause a lot of damage.
(B) Scientists aren't always right, but this theory makes sense.
(C) Scientists continue to do research and find new evidence to prove the plate tectonic theory.
(D) Someday, the earth might be all one continent, or all countries could be their own continent.

Sentence Construction

Read this rough draft of a student's essay. Then answer the questions.

(1) Last year, my father threw a surprise birthday party for my mother. (2) All of her friends and family were there. (3) It was a great night. (4) The days leading up to the party were not so great.

(5) I am terrible at keeping secrets. (6) I crack easily under the pressure. (7) My mother knows this. (8) She came right to me when she suspected something was up. (9) She asked me if Dad was planning something for her birthday. (10) She looked me right in the eye and smiled.

(11) What was I supposed to do? (12) Think about it. (13) I couldn't lie to my mother! (14) So instead I took a big gulp of my water and pretended it went down the wrong pipe. (15) I coughed and eventually excused myself from the room.

(16) Then, my father asked me to hide some of the decorations under my bed. (17) Of course, the next day, my mother made me clean my room. (18) She said if I didn't do it, then she would do it herself. (19) Unfortunately I had to clean it. (20) And make it good enough for her to not check under the bed. (21) Or in the closet.

(22) When the big day finally arrived, I couldn't have been more excited or more nervous. (23) We were pretty sure that she didn't know what was going on. (24) However, we still had to get through the day and get her to the party without revealing the secret.

(25) I almost messed up again when I suggested that she wear her diamond earrings because Grandma likes the way they look on her. (26) This made my mother raise an eyebrow and ask why it mattered whether Grandma liked them it was not like she was going to see them. (27) Dad saved me by reminding Mom that Grandma has great fashion sense.

(28) In the end, the party went well. (29) Keeping the surprise party a secret was hard, but it was well worth it to see the look of shock on Mom's face when everyone jumped out in the restaurant.

1. Which word **best** combines sentences 3 and 4?
   Ⓐ and
   Ⓑ so
   Ⓒ because
   Ⓓ but

2. Which sentence is an interrogative sentence?
   Ⓐ sentence 10
   Ⓑ sentence 11
   Ⓒ sentence 12
   Ⓓ sentence 13

3. Which sentence is an exclamatory sentence?
   Ⓐ sentence 10
   Ⓑ sentence 11
   Ⓒ sentence 12
   Ⓓ sentence 13

4. Which sentence is an imperative sentence?
   Ⓐ sentence 10
   Ⓑ sentence 11
   Ⓒ sentence 12
   Ⓓ sentence 13

5. Which sentence is a declarative sentence?
   Ⓐ sentence 10
   Ⓑ sentence 11
   Ⓒ sentence 12
   Ⓓ sentence 13

6. Which sentence is a run-on sentence?
   Ⓐ sentence 25
   Ⓑ sentence 26
   Ⓒ sentence 27
   Ⓓ sentence 28

7. Which sentence is an incomplete sentence?
   Ⓐ sentence 21
   Ⓑ sentence 22
   Ⓒ sentence 23
   Ⓓ sentence 24

8. Which word **best** combines sentences 7 and 8?
   Ⓐ but
   Ⓑ so
   Ⓒ however
   Ⓓ or

9. What is the subject of sentence 2?
   Ⓐ all
   Ⓑ friends
   Ⓒ family
   Ⓓ there

10. Which sentence has a compound predicate?
    Ⓐ sentence 15
    Ⓑ sentence 16
    Ⓒ sentence 17
    Ⓓ sentence 18

Grammar

Choose the best way to write the underlined parts of each sentence.

1. Bill <u>has enjoyed</u> going to summer camp at Lake Tanaka last year.
   - Ⓐ had enjoyed
   - Ⓑ will have enjoyed
   - Ⓒ have enjoyed
   - Ⓓ correct as is

2. Next week, my parents <u>will had known</u> each other for 30 years.
   - Ⓐ will have known
   - Ⓑ had known
   - Ⓒ has known
   - Ⓓ correct as is

3. I read that book because you <u>had recommended</u> it.
   - Ⓐ has recommended
   - Ⓑ had recommend
   - Ⓒ will have recommended
   - Ⓓ correct as is

4. No one <u>has ever saw</u> me hit the ball over the net in volleyball.
   - Ⓐ have ever saw
   - Ⓑ has ever seen
   - Ⓒ have ever seen
   - Ⓓ correct as is

5. Everyone <u>are going</u> on a field trip to the zoo tomorrow.
   - Ⓐ was going
   - Ⓑ be going
   - Ⓒ is going
   - Ⓓ correct as is

6. Someone <u>has wrote</u> graffiti on the wall in the bathroom.
   - Ⓐ has written
   - Ⓑ have written
   - Ⓒ have wrote
   - Ⓓ correct as is

7. All of us <u>have prepared</u> for the big game tomorrow.
   - Ⓐ had prepared
   - Ⓑ has prepared
   - Ⓒ have prepare
   - Ⓓ correct as is

8. Some of the students <u>have told</u> their parents about the field trip.
   - Ⓐ has told
   - Ⓑ have telled
   - Ⓒ has telled
   - Ⓓ correct as is

9. My brother and sister <u>have bought their</u> holiday gifts already.
   - Ⓐ has bought
   - Ⓑ have buyed
   - Ⓒ has buyed
   - Ⓓ correct as is

10. My mother and father <u>has raised</u> us to be responsible.
    - Ⓐ have raised
    - Ⓑ has risen
    - Ⓒ have risen
    - Ⓓ correct as is

11. Many people <u>have wrote</u> stories about pirates and buried treasure.
    - Ⓐ have write
    - Ⓑ has written
    - Ⓒ have written
    - Ⓓ correct as is

12. <u>Them</u> went to the amusement park together last weekend.
    - Ⓐ Us
    - Ⓑ Me
    - Ⓒ They
    - Ⓓ correct as is

13. The food in the cafeteria today was <u>different</u> <u>than</u> what they served yesterday.
    - Ⓐ different from
    - Ⓑ different to
    - Ⓒ different among
    - Ⓓ correct as is

14. He <u>could of kept</u> them all for himself.
    - Ⓐ could have keeped
    - Ⓑ could of keeped
    - Ⓒ could have kept
    - Ⓓ correct as is

15. My cat <u>have caught</u> this mouse.
    - Ⓐ has caught
    - Ⓑ have catched
    - Ⓒ has catched
    - Ⓓ correct as is

16. My mother or my grandparents <u>have told</u> me this story before.
    - Ⓐ has told
    - Ⓑ have telled
    - Ⓒ has telled
    - Ⓓ correct as is

17. We went to <u>Jons</u> house after school.
    - Ⓐ Jon
    - Ⓑ Jons'
    - Ⓒ Jon's
    - Ⓓ correct as is

18. The different <u>communities'</u> efforts have made this city a great place to live.
    - Ⓐ communitie's
    - Ⓑ communities
    - Ⓒ communitys'
    - Ⓓ correct as is

Punctuation

Decide which underlined part in each sentence contains an error in punctuation. Darken the circle for the letter that matches your answer. If there is no mistake, then darken the circle for *No Mistake*.

1. My mother <u>asked,</u> "Can you get some <u>bread,</u> and eggs on your way home from <u>school?"</u>
Ⓐ Ⓑ Ⓒ

<u>No mistake</u>
Ⓓ

2. I <u>didn't</u> want to go to the school <u>dance;</u> I don't like to <u>dance.</u> <u>No mistake</u>
Ⓐ Ⓑ Ⓒ Ⓓ

3. <u>Tonight</u> <u>Louis,</u> can you help me make <u>dinner?</u> <u>No mistake</u>
Ⓐ Ⓑ Ⓒ Ⓓ

4. By the beginning of first <u>grade</u> most students already know about <u>6,000</u> <u>words.</u> <u>No mistake</u>
Ⓐ Ⓑ Ⓒ Ⓓ

5. <u>Yesterday,</u> the squirrel found some <u>nuts,</u> took <u>them,</u> and ate them. <u>No mistake</u>
Ⓐ Ⓑ Ⓒ Ⓓ

6. Thomas Edison was born on <u>February,</u> <u>11,</u> <u>1847.</u> <u>No mistake</u>
Ⓐ Ⓑ Ⓒ Ⓓ

7. Have you ever been to <u>Providence,</u> Rhode <u>Island,</u> in the <u>fall.</u> <u>No mistake</u>
Ⓐ Ⓑ Ⓒ Ⓓ

8. <u>Oh</u> I thought <u>I'd</u> surprise <u>you!</u> <u>No mistake</u>
Ⓐ Ⓑ Ⓒ Ⓓ

Read the questions below and choose the best answer.

9. Read the sentence below. After which word should a semicolon be placed?

I don't eat steak in fact, I'm a vegetarian.

Ⓐ don't
Ⓑ eat
Ⓒ steak
Ⓓ I'm

10. Read the sentence below. After which word should a semicolon be placed?

Mrs. Joleson is our principal Mr. Larks is our assistant principal.

Ⓐ Joleson
Ⓑ our
Ⓒ principal
Ⓓ Larks

11. Read the sentence below. After which word should a comma be placed?

Since the weather is getting worse we should cancel the picnic.

Ⓐ Since
Ⓑ weather
Ⓒ getting
Ⓓ worse

12. Read the sentence below. After which word should a comma be placed?

If you want to see Cheryl call her on the telephone.

Ⓐ you
Ⓑ Cheryl
Ⓒ call
Ⓓ her

13. Read the sentence below. What is the correct way to write the underlined word?

"Do you want to go fishing with <u>me</u>" Dad asked.

Ⓐ me?"
Ⓑ me,"
Ⓒ me."
Ⓓ correct as is

14. Read the sentence below. What is the correct way to write the underlined words?

My older <u>sister Kayla</u> is home from college for the summer.

Ⓐ sister, Kayla
Ⓑ sister, Kayla,
Ⓒ sister Kayla,
Ⓓ correct as is

15. Read the sentence below. What is the correct way to write the underlined words?

The dance is scheduled for <u>Wednesday June 18,</u> at 7 PM.

Ⓐ Wednesday, June 18
Ⓑ Wednesday, June, 18,
Ⓒ Wednesday June, 18
Ⓓ correct as is

16. Read the sentence below. What is the correct way to write the underlined words?

My family is going to India for a <u>month, but I</u> want to stay here.

Ⓐ month, but,
Ⓑ month but
Ⓒ month; but
Ⓓ correct as is

Capitalization

Answer the questions below.

1. Read the sentence below. What is the correct way to write the underlined words?

The Everglades National Park, in Florida, is the largest subtropical wilderness in the United States.

Ⓐ Everglades national Park, in Florida
Ⓑ Everglades National park, in Florida
Ⓒ Everglades national park, in Florida
Ⓓ correct as is

2. Read the sentence below. What is the correct way to write the underlined words?

My cousin got an apartment on Oak drive.

Ⓐ Oak Drive
Ⓑ oak Drive
Ⓒ oak drive
Ⓓ correct as is

3. Read the sentence below. What is the correct way to write the underlined words?

locust valley hospital is getting a new wing.

Ⓐ locust valley Hospital
Ⓑ Locust Valley Hospital
Ⓒ Locust Valley hospital
Ⓓ correct as is

4. Read the sentence below. What is the correct way to write the underlined words?

I enjoyed reading the short story "the Tell Tale Heart."

Ⓐ The Tell-Tale Heart
Ⓑ the tell-tale heart
Ⓒ the Tell-Tale heart
Ⓓ correct as is

5. Read the sentence below. What is the correct way to write the underlined words?

I wonder who will be the president of the united states when I am 50.

Ⓐ President of the united states
Ⓑ President of the United states
Ⓒ president of the United States
Ⓓ correct as is

6. Read the sentence below. What is the correct way to write the underlined words?

My teacher, Mr. Lopez, always tells the class, "practice makes perfect."

Ⓐ Practice makes perfect
Ⓑ practice Makes perfect
Ⓒ practice makes Perfect
Ⓓ correct as is

7. Read the sentence below. Which word should be capitalized?

If i'd had the chance, I would have gone to camp last summer.

Ⓐ I'd
Ⓑ Camp
Ⓒ Summer
Ⓓ none of the above

8. Read the sentence below. Which word should be capitalized?

My grandparents are coming to visit us on thanksgiving.

Ⓐ Grandparents
Ⓑ Us
Ⓒ Thanksgiving
Ⓓ none of the above

9. Read the sentence below. Which word should be capitalized?

he said his favorite color was blue, so I bought him a blue shirt.

Ⓐ He
Ⓑ His
Ⓒ Blue
Ⓓ none of the above

10. Read the sentence below. Which word should be capitalized?

Emile asked, "where is the town library?"

Ⓐ Where
Ⓑ Town
Ⓒ Library
Ⓓ none of the above

11. Read the sentence below. Which word should be capitalized?

Kendra visited three national parks last summer.

Ⓐ National
Ⓑ Parks
Ⓒ Summer
Ⓓ none of the above

12. Read the sentence below. Which word should be capitalized?

Sal and i are on the same baseball team.

Ⓐ Team
Ⓑ I
Ⓒ Baseball
Ⓓ none of the above

13. Read the sentence below. Which word should be capitalized?

I asked dad if we were going on vacation this summer.

Ⓐ Going
Ⓑ Summer
Ⓒ Dad
Ⓓ none of the above

14. Read the sentence below. Which word should be capitalized?

Rick and Angie were married in a small town in Costa Rica.

Ⓐ Small
Ⓑ Town
Ⓒ Married
Ⓓ none of the above

Spelling

Choose the word that is spelled correctly in each group.

1. Ⓐ temperture
   Ⓑ tempiture
   Ⓒ tempaher
   Ⓓ temperature

2. Ⓐ scheduale
   Ⓑ schedule
   Ⓒ scedual
   Ⓓ scheduel

3. Ⓐ promis
   Ⓑ promiss
   Ⓒ promise
   Ⓓ promese

4. Ⓐ consiterate
   Ⓑ considorate
   Ⓒ considerate
   Ⓓ conseterate

5. Ⓐ posponement
   Ⓑ postponment
   Ⓒ postponmint
   Ⓓ postponement

6. Ⓐ produciton
   Ⓑ production
   Ⓒ perduction
   Ⓓ praduction

7. Ⓐ critisize
   Ⓑ criticize
   Ⓒ critasize
   Ⓓ critsize

8. Ⓐ remedial
   Ⓑ remedyal
   Ⓒ rimedyal
   Ⓓ remedeal

9. Ⓐ tommorow
   Ⓑ tomarrow
   Ⓒ tommorrow
   Ⓓ tomorrow

10. Ⓐ destinastion
    Ⓑ destenation
    Ⓒ destination
    Ⓓ distenation

11. (A) banana
     (B) banna
     (C) bannana
     (D) bananna

12. (A) bufay
     (B) bufet
     (C) buffet
     (D) buffay

13. (A) egnore
     (B) ignor
     (C) ignore
     (D) eggnor

14. (A) dissurb
     (B) distrub
     (C) destrub
     (D) disturb

15. (A) deduction
     (B) dedudion
     (C) deduciton
     (D) deduckshon

16. (A) pattren
     (B) pattern
     (C) patern
     (D) patturn

17. (A) kindergarden
     (B) kindigarten
     (C) kindergarten
     (D) kindegarten

18. (A) vegetable
     (B) vegtable
     (C) vegetible
     (D) vegible

19. (A) appologize
     (B) appologise
     (C) apologize
     (D) appolojise

20. (A) autograph
     (B) atograph
     (C) otagraph
     (D) autegraph

Vocabulary

Answer the questions.

1. Which French expression would be **most** appropriate to say to someone about to eat a meal?
- Ⓐ Bon appétit!
- Ⓑ Merci beaucoup!
- Ⓒ Bon voyage!
- Ⓓ A la carte!

2. Read the sentence below. What is the meaning of the underlined word?

My mother decided not to drive her car after we saw an unknown pool of fluid underneath it.
- Ⓐ a liquid
- Ⓑ readily reshaped
- Ⓒ smooth and flowing
- Ⓓ convertible into cash

3. *Ordinary* means *common* in the same way that *unusual* means _____.
- Ⓐ common
- Ⓑ rare
- Ⓒ normal
- Ⓓ universal

4. *Classroom* is to *lesson* as *courtroom* is to _____.
- Ⓐ judge
- Ⓑ jury
- Ⓒ trial
- Ⓓ idea

5. Read the sentence below. What is the meaning of the underlined word?

The senator is trying to ensure passage of the energy conservation bill.
- Ⓐ the act or process of passing
- Ⓑ a journey
- Ⓒ part of a written work
- Ⓓ approval of a law by a legislative body

6. Read the sentence below. Without changing the meaning of the sentence, which word can **best** replace the underlined word?

Palo hammered the damaged fender back into shape.
- Ⓐ bruised
- Ⓑ tattered
- Ⓒ dented
- Ⓓ scratched

7. Read the sentence below. What two words **best** fit this sentence?

_____ is the _____ of the World War II memorial.
- Ⓐ Hear, site
- Ⓑ Here, site
- Ⓒ Hear, sight
- Ⓓ Here, sight

8. Read the sentence below. What is the meaning of the underlined word?

All of the good restaurants are in this quarter of town.
- Ⓐ any of four equal parts into which something can be divided
- Ⓑ a coin in the United States or Canada worth 25 cents
- Ⓒ one of four time periods that make up a sports game
- Ⓓ a district or section of a city

9. Read the sentence below. Without changing the meaning of the sentence, which word can **best** replace the underlined word?

> Leanne carved a <u>small</u> model of a soldier out of wood.

Ⓐ tiny
Ⓑ miniature
Ⓒ minor
Ⓓ microscopic

10. Read the sentence below. Which French phrase meaning "with ice cream" can be used to complete this sentence?

> After dinner, we told the waitress we would like some apple pie
>
> _____.

Ⓐ à la carte
Ⓑ à la mode
Ⓒ au gratin
Ⓓ crème brûlée

11. Which word means "to avoid" or "duck"?
Ⓐ discontinue
Ⓑ shirk
Ⓒ bawl
Ⓓ tilt

12. Which word from the Latin root "mit," ("to send"), means "to send through or allow"?
Ⓐ transmit
Ⓑ submit
Ⓒ permit
Ⓓ admit

13. Read the sentence below. Without changing the meaning of the sentence, which word can **best** replace the underlined word?

> Sarah's <u>unique</u> bracelet was a gift from her friend's recent trip to India.

Ⓐ colorful
Ⓑ distinctive
Ⓒ careful
Ⓓ unattractive

14. Read the sentence below. What is the meaning of the underlined word?

> Mr. Hansen's briefcase, <u>laden</u> with heavy books, slowed the teacher down.

Ⓐ effective
Ⓑ energetic
Ⓒ handmade
Ⓓ filled

15. Read the sentence below. Which word meaning "ball" or "globe" can be used to complete this sentence?

> Beth's project for the science fair included a large foam _____ to represent the earth.

Ⓐ imprint
Ⓑ pillar
Ⓒ sphere
Ⓓ continent

16. Read the sentence below. Which Spanish word meaning "a public exhibition of cowboy skills" can be used to complete the sentence?

> When we visited my aunt in New Mexico, she took us to see a _____, where my uncle was roping calves.

Ⓐ lasso
Ⓑ corral
Ⓒ bronco
Ⓓ rodeo

Section 3: Test

Read the passage and answer the questions.

Unique New York

Say the phrase "unique New York" three times fast. Did you find that you can't say it correctly more than once or twice? It becomes jumbled, doesn't it? Try saying it ten times fast. "Unique New York" becomes "unique You Nork" or something similar.

"Unique New York" and other tongue twisters reveal an interesting phenomenon. Every language has them, though they differ from language to language. Why do people have this problem with certain phrases?

When it comes to speech, the tongue is the tool for accuracy. It can move in a number of ways, like pressing against the back of your top front teeth when you make a /t/ sound. Notice that your tongue moves away as soon as you finish the /t/ sound. Try keeping your tongue pressed against the back of your front teeth while you make a /t/ sound—it won't do it. Your tongue is very precise.

However, your tongue has its limitations. This makes us ask, is it your tongue or your brain that makes you not able to say tongue twisters? Some studies point to the brain as the culprit. One such study found that it takes us longer to silently read sentences with tongue twisters than sentences without. If our tongue was at fault, we would still be able to read the tongue twisters in our head.

Whatever the cause, don't beat yourself up about getting tongue-tied over "unique New York." You're probably still a very good speaker. The average person makes only about one error per every thousand words spoken—though just reading this passage probably hurt that average!

1. Why did the author write this passage?
Ⓐ to persuade readers to visit New York
Ⓑ to encourage readers to say tongue twisters
Ⓒ to inform readers about why we get tongue-tied
Ⓓ to entertain readers with silly phrases

2. What has made some scientists conclude that the brain is responsible for getting tongue-tied over tongue twisters?
Ⓐ They said "unique New York" ten times fast accurately.
Ⓑ A study showed we can't read tongue twisters well either.
Ⓒ Our tongues stay against our teeth when saying a /t/ sound.
Ⓓ The brain is more powerful than the tongue.

3. According to the passage, about how many errors would you make if you spoke two thousand words?
Ⓐ one
Ⓑ two
Ⓒ three
Ⓓ four

4. Where would this passage **most likely** be found?
Ⓐ in a magazine for young readers
Ⓑ on the front page of a newspaper
Ⓒ in an anatomy textbook
Ⓓ in a book about New York

5. Read the sentence from the passage below. What does the word *precise* mean?
Your tongue is very precise.
Ⓐ exact
Ⓑ precious
Ⓒ careful
Ⓓ approximate

6. What does the phrase "beat yourself up" in the last paragraph mean?
Ⓐ hit yourself on the head
Ⓑ bite your tongue
Ⓒ get upset
Ⓓ hit someone else

7. Which source would probably provide the **best** information on this topic?
Ⓐ a book of tongue twisters
Ⓑ a science book
Ⓒ a website about New York
Ⓓ a psychology textbook

8. What does the author imply in this passage?
Ⓐ Everyone can say tongue twisters easily.
Ⓑ New York is not as unique as people think.
Ⓒ Our brains have nothing to do with tongue twisters.
Ⓓ Most people have trouble saying tongue twisters.

Madeleine is writing a letter to her sister, who is away at college.
Read her first draft below. Then answer the questions.

Dear Angie,

(1) How is college going. (2) I can't believe you been gone for two weeks already. (3) I didn't think I would miss you, but I do. (4) I hope you miss me too. (5) When you come home I want to go to the movies get some ice cream and talk to you about college. (6) You hasn't missed much around hear. (7) Mom forgets that you're gone sometimes. (8) She sets a place for you at the table. (9) We had meatloaf last night for dinner. (10) Since you'll be gone for a while, I can have your room? (11) Its a lot bigger than mine. (12) We'll discuss it. (13) When you come home for Thanksgiving. (14) You better write me back soon!

Love always,
Madeleine (your sister)

9. How is sentence 1 **best** written?
Ⓐ How is college going?
Ⓑ How college is going.
Ⓒ How college going?
Ⓓ correct as is

10. How is sentence 2 **best** written?
Ⓐ I can't believe you been gone for two weeks already?
Ⓑ I can't believe you have been gone for two weeks already.
Ⓒ I can't believe you have been gone for too weeks already.
Ⓓ correct as is

11. How is sentence 3 **best** written?
Ⓐ I didn't think I would miss you but I do.
Ⓑ I didn't think I would miss you but, I do.
Ⓒ I didn't think, I would miss you, but I do.
Ⓓ correct as is

12. How is sentence 5 **best** written?
Ⓐ When you come home: I want to go to the movies; get some ice cream; and talk to you about college.
Ⓑ When you come home I want to go to the movies, get some ice cream, and talk to you about college.
Ⓒ When you come home, I want to go to the movies, get some ice cream, and talk to you about college.
Ⓓ correct as is

13. How is sentence 6 **best** written?
  ⒶYou hasn't missed much around here.
  ⒷYou haven't missed much around here.
  ⒸYou haven't missed much around hear.
  Ⓓcorrect as is

14. How can sentences 7 and 8 **best** be combined without changing their meaning?
  ⒶMom forgets that you're gone sometimes and sets a place for you at the table.
  ⒷMom forgets that you're gone sometimes, but she sets a place for you at the table.
  ⒸMom forgets that you're gone sometimes, or she sets a place for you at the table.
  ⒹMom forgets that you're gone sometimes; because she sets a place for you at the table.

15. How is sentence 10 **best** written?
  ⒶSince you'll be gone for a while, I can have your room.
  ⒷSince you'll be gone for a while, can I have your room?
  ⒸSince you'll be gone for a while; can I have your room?
  Ⓓcorrect as is

16. Which sentence doesn't belong in Madeleine's letter?
  Ⓐsentence 4
  Ⓑsentence 6
  Ⓒsentence 8
  Ⓓsentence 9

17. What punctuation is missing from sentence 11?
  Ⓐquotation marks
  Ⓑsemicolon
  Ⓒapostrophe
  Ⓓcomma

18. Read the sentence from the letter below. Where would be the **best** place to add this sentence?
  I think about you a lot.
  Ⓐafter sentence 2
  Ⓑafter sentence 6
  Ⓒafter sentence 8
  Ⓓafter sentence 10

19. Which sentence is an incomplete thought?
  Ⓐsentence 10
  Ⓑsentence 11
  Ⓒsentence 12
  Ⓓsentence 13

20. If Madeleine wants to find a synonym for *bigger* in sentence 11, where should she look?
  Ⓐthe dictionary
  Ⓑan encyclopedia
  Ⓒa thesaurus
  Ⓓa newspaper

Comparing and Ordering Numbers

Answer the questions below.

1. Which point shows the location of $\frac{5}{2}$ on the number line?

A number line:
0   A   1   B   2   C   3   D   4

Ⓐ point A
Ⓑ point B
Ⓒ point C
Ⓓ point D

2. Which list of numbers is ordered from greatest to least?

Ⓐ 4, $4\frac{1}{4}$, .4, .04
Ⓑ $4\frac{1}{4}$, 4, .4, .04
Ⓒ .04, .4, 4, $4\frac{1}{4}$
Ⓓ 4, .4, .04, $4\frac{1}{4}$

3. Which of the following fractions is closest to 2?

Ⓐ $\frac{5}{4}$
Ⓑ $\frac{5}{6}$
Ⓒ $\frac{5}{2}$
Ⓓ $\frac{5}{3}$

4. ____ > 2

Ⓐ $\frac{3}{2}$
Ⓑ $\frac{4}{3}$
Ⓒ $\frac{9}{4}$
Ⓓ $\frac{6}{3}$

5. Which is the smallest number: $-\frac{5}{8}, \frac{2}{8}, 1\frac{3}{8}, \frac{4}{8}$?

Ⓐ $-\frac{5}{8}$
Ⓑ $\frac{2}{8}$
Ⓒ $1\frac{3}{8}$
Ⓓ $\frac{4}{8}$

6. Which is the largest number: .099, .0099, .999, 9.9999?

Ⓐ 0.099
Ⓑ 0.0099
Ⓒ 0.999
Ⓓ 9.9999

7. Which list of numbers is ordered from least to greatest?

Ⓐ 21,121; 22,211; 21,212; 22,221
Ⓑ 22,221; 22,211; 21,212; 21,121
Ⓒ 21,121; 21,212; 22,211; 22,221
Ⓓ 21,121; 21,212; 22,221; 22,211

8. Which of the following decimals is closest to 0?

Ⓐ −.055
Ⓑ .125
Ⓒ −.505
Ⓓ .251

Estimating

Answer the questions below.

1. Jackson spent $56.89, $18.80, $42.40, and $38.95 on gifts for his family. Which is the **best** estimate for the total amount that he spent?
   - Ⓐ $180
   - Ⓑ $170
   - Ⓒ $160
   - Ⓓ $150

2. Holly gets paid about $1,450 each month. What is a reasonable estimate of how much she makes in a year?
   - Ⓐ less than $10,000
   - Ⓑ between $10,000 and $15,000
   - Ⓒ between $15,000 and $20,000
   - Ⓓ more than $20,000

3. The Martinsons traveled 3,476 miles in 9 days. Each day they traveled about the same number of miles. What is a good estimate of how many miles they traveled each day?
   - Ⓐ 200 miles
   - Ⓑ 300 miles
   - Ⓒ 400 miles
   - Ⓓ 500 miles

4. About how much is 78×3 ?
   - Ⓐ 210
   - Ⓑ 240
   - Ⓒ 280
   - Ⓓ 320

5. About how much is $3,585 \div 40$?
   - Ⓐ 80
   - Ⓑ 800
   - Ⓒ 90
   - Ⓓ 900

6. If a candy bar costs $1.49, then about how much would it cost to buy 4 candy bars?
   - Ⓐ $4.00
   - Ⓑ $5.00
   - Ⓒ $5.50
   - Ⓓ $6.00

Use the chart below to answer questions 7–9.

Item	Price
Salad	$2.35
Hamburger	$5.89
Fruit Cup	$3.45
Chicken Sandwich	$6.79
Juice	$0.69

7. About how much would a hamburger, salad, and juice cost?
   - Ⓐ $9.00
   - Ⓑ $8.00
   - Ⓒ $10.00
   - Ⓓ $7.00

8. About how much more does a chicken sandwich cost than a fruit cup?
   - Ⓐ $2.00
   - Ⓑ $3.00
   - Ⓒ $6.00
   - Ⓓ $5.00

9. About how much less does a salad cost than a hamburger?
   - Ⓐ $7.00
   - Ⓑ $2.00
   - Ⓒ $3.00
   - Ⓓ $4.00

Greatest Common Factor and Least Common Multiple

Answer the questions below.

1. What is the GCF of 12 and 27?
- Ⓐ 3
- Ⓑ 4
- Ⓒ 9
- Ⓓ 12

2. What is the LCM of 6 and 30?
- Ⓐ 2
- Ⓑ 6
- Ⓒ 30
- Ⓓ 180

3. What is the GCF of 54 and 72?
- Ⓐ 72
- Ⓑ 54
- Ⓒ 18
- Ⓓ 9

4. What is the LCM of 12 and 18?
- Ⓐ 6
- Ⓑ 12
- Ⓒ 18
- Ⓓ 36

5. The GCF of what two numbers is 12?
- Ⓐ 12 and 16
- Ⓑ 48 and 60
- Ⓒ 18 and 36
- Ⓓ 4 and 6

6. The LCM of what two numbers is 36?
- Ⓐ 6 and 12
- Ⓑ 12 and 18
- Ⓒ 3 and 12
- Ⓓ 4 and 6

7. The GCF of what two numbers is 15?
- Ⓐ 15 and 75
- Ⓑ 30 and 60
- Ⓒ 60 and 90
- Ⓓ 5 and 10

8. The LCM of what two numbers is 18?
- Ⓐ 3 and 6
- Ⓑ 6 and 9
- Ⓒ 4 and 18
- Ⓓ 4 and 36

9. What two numbers have an LCM of 36 and a GCF of 3?
- Ⓐ 3 and 36
- Ⓑ 6 and 12
- Ⓒ 9 and 16
- Ⓓ 12 and 36

10. What two numbers have an LCM of 24 and a GCF of 2?
- Ⓐ 4 and 8
- Ⓑ 4 and 6
- Ⓒ 3 and 4
- Ⓓ 6 and 8

11. What is the LCM of 2, 6, and 7?
- Ⓐ 12
- Ⓑ 36
- Ⓒ 42
- Ⓓ 84

12. What is the GCF of 16, 24, and 32?
- Ⓐ 8
- Ⓑ 12
- Ⓒ 24
- Ⓓ 48

Proportions

Answer the questions below.

1. $\frac{2}{5} = \frac{6}{x}$, when $x = ?$
Ⓐ 10
Ⓑ 15
Ⓒ 18
Ⓓ 20

2. Billy has 7 marbles. Three of the marbles are red. What is the ratio of red marbles to total marbles?
Ⓐ 3:4
Ⓑ 3:7
Ⓒ 4:3
Ⓓ 7:3

3. A bus drove 70 miles in 2 hours. What is the unit rate?
Ⓐ 35 miles / 1 hour
Ⓑ 70 miles / 2 hours
Ⓒ 140 miles / 1 hour
Ⓓ 140 miles / 4 hours

4. Catherine is making a model of a building. She wants to make it a scale of 100:1. If the building is 250 feet tall, then how tall should Catherine's model be?
Ⓐ 25 feet
Ⓑ 15 feet
Ⓒ 2.5 feet
Ⓓ 1 foot

5. $\frac{x}{8} = \frac{15}{24}$, when $x = ?$
Ⓐ 10
Ⓑ 45
Ⓒ 12
Ⓓ 5

6. If you get an extra life in a video game every 15,000 points, then how many points do you need to score to get 5 lives?
Ⓐ 75,000
Ⓑ 60,000
Ⓒ 50,000
Ⓓ 45,000

7. A mother dog has a litter of 12 puppies. If $\frac{2}{3}$ of the puppies are brown, then how many puppies are **not** brown?
Ⓐ 3
Ⓑ 4
Ⓒ 6
Ⓓ 8

8. Hillary wants to make some extra money for the winter by shoveling snow from people's driveways. For every 100 ft² of driveway that Hillary shovels, she charges $8. How much would she make from a driveway that is 325 ft²?
Ⓐ $12.50
Ⓑ $18.00
Ⓒ $26.00
Ⓓ $28.00

9. $\frac{2}{x} = \frac{14}{21}$, when $x =$
Ⓐ 3
Ⓑ 7
Ⓒ 5
Ⓓ 9

Fractions

Answer the questions below.

1. $\frac{3}{4} + \frac{1}{2} =$

Ⓐ $\frac{2}{3}$

Ⓑ $1\frac{1}{4}$

Ⓒ $1\frac{1}{2}$

Ⓓ $3\frac{1}{2}$

2. Which fraction is equivalent to $\frac{6}{18}$?

Ⓐ $\frac{2}{3}$

Ⓑ $\frac{1}{4}$

Ⓒ $\frac{1}{3}$

Ⓓ $\frac{3}{4}$

3. Which set of fractions is in order from least to greatest?

Ⓐ $\frac{1}{2}, \frac{1}{3}, \frac{1}{5}, \frac{1}{6}$

Ⓑ $\frac{3}{5}, \frac{1}{3}, \frac{4}{5}, \frac{2}{3}$

Ⓒ $\frac{2}{12}, \frac{1}{5}, \frac{3}{12}, \frac{2}{4}$

Ⓓ $\frac{2}{9}, \frac{2}{10}, \frac{1}{3}, \frac{2}{3}$

4. Which decimal is equivalent to $\frac{3}{4}$?

Ⓐ 0.75

Ⓑ 0.67

Ⓒ 0.34

Ⓓ 1.33

5. $\frac{2}{3} \times \frac{1}{4} =$

Ⓐ $\frac{8}{3}$

Ⓑ $\frac{3}{8}$

Ⓒ $\frac{2}{12}$

Ⓓ $\frac{1}{6}$

6. What is $\frac{2}{3}$ of 120?

Ⓐ 80

Ⓑ 40

Ⓒ 200

Ⓓ 160

7. $\frac{4}{6} - \frac{1}{8} =$

Ⓐ $\frac{5}{8}$

Ⓑ $\frac{13}{24}$

Ⓒ $\frac{5}{24}$

Ⓓ $\frac{3}{6}$

8. Jessica weighs 80 lbs. Her older brother weighs $\frac{3}{4}$ more than her. How much does her brother weigh?

Ⓐ 60 lbs

Ⓑ 100 lbs

Ⓒ 120 lbs

Ⓓ 140 lbs

9. What fraction of the circle is shaded?

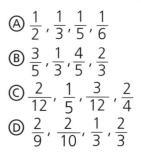

Ⓐ $\frac{1}{4}$

Ⓑ $\frac{1}{2}$

Ⓒ $\frac{1}{6}$

Ⓓ $\frac{1}{3}$

10. $3 \div \frac{3}{8} =$

(A) $\frac{13}{24}$

(B) 8

(C) $\frac{24}{9}$

(D) $\frac{9}{24}$

11. Which set of fractions is in order from least to greatest?

(A) $\frac{2}{3}, \frac{5}{6}, \frac{6}{10}, \frac{3}{4}$

(B) $\frac{2}{6}, \frac{5}{10}, \frac{2}{3}, \frac{9}{11}$

(C) $\frac{10}{11}, \frac{4}{7}, \frac{2}{5}, \frac{1}{3}$

(D) $\frac{3}{8}, \frac{3}{9}, \frac{3}{10}, \frac{3}{11}$

12. $\frac{5}{9} - \frac{1}{3} =$

(A) $\frac{4}{6}$

(B) $\frac{2}{3}$

(C) $\frac{2}{9}$

(D) $\frac{4}{9}$

13. The improper fraction $\frac{25}{12}$ is equivalent to which mixed number?

(A) $2\frac{1}{25}$

(B) $1\frac{11}{12}$

(C) $3\frac{1}{12}$

(D) $2\frac{1}{12}$

14. $7\frac{1}{6} + 2\frac{7}{18} =$

(A) $9\frac{5}{9}$

(B) $9\frac{1}{3}$

(C) $23\frac{5}{9}$

(D) $9\frac{13}{18}$

15. 95 is $\frac{3}{5}$ of which number?

(A) 57

(B) $237\frac{1}{2}$

(C) $158\frac{1}{3}$

(D) 38

16. Which decimal is equivalent to $\frac{1}{8}$?

(A) 0.25

(B) 0.125

(C) 0.8

(D) 1.8

17. $6\frac{1}{3} \times 9\frac{2}{5} =$

(A) $59\frac{8}{15}$

(B) $54\frac{2}{15}$

(C) $831\frac{2}{15}$

(D) $22\frac{4}{5}$

18. Which set of numbers is in order from greatest to least?

(A) $\frac{9}{22}, \frac{7}{12}, \frac{2}{3}, \frac{7}{9}$

(B) $\frac{9}{22}, \frac{7}{12}, \frac{7}{9}, \frac{2}{3}$

(C) $\frac{2}{3}, \frac{7}{9}, \frac{9}{22}, \frac{7}{12}$

(D) $\frac{7}{9}, \frac{2}{3}, \frac{7}{12}, \frac{9}{22}$

Percentages

Answer the questions below.

1. What is 40% of 300?
- Ⓐ 7.5
- Ⓑ 15
- Ⓒ 120
- Ⓓ 140

2. 90 is 9% of what number?
- Ⓐ 100
- Ⓑ 90
- Ⓒ 900
- Ⓓ 1,000

3. What percentage of 20 is 5?
- Ⓐ 400
- Ⓑ 20
- Ⓒ 25
- Ⓓ 75

4. If the average tip for a waitress is 15%, then how much should you tip if the bill is $36.00?
- Ⓐ $2.40
- Ⓑ $5.40
- Ⓒ $0.24
- Ⓓ $0.54

5. Sheila runs 60% of a 3-mile-long track in 20 minutes. How far did she run?
- Ⓐ 1.8 miles
- Ⓑ 1.2 miles
- Ⓒ 0.5 miles
- Ⓓ 1.5 miles

6. Sam wants to buy a toy for $40. He has a coupon for 20% off. How much will Sam have to pay for the toy if there is no tax?
- Ⓐ $8
- Ⓑ $26
- Ⓒ $32
- Ⓓ $36

7. What is 35% of 250?
- Ⓐ 87.5
- Ⓑ 714
- Ⓒ 71.4
- Ⓓ 8.75

8. Everything on Planet Z loses 25% of its weight on earth. How much will you weigh on Planet Z if you weigh 80 lb on earth?
- Ⓐ 20 lb
- Ⓑ 45 lb
- Ⓒ 55 lb
- Ⓓ 60 lb

9. Which of the following is the largest amount?
- Ⓐ 30% of 270
- Ⓑ 50% of 590
- Ⓒ 70% of 400
- Ⓓ 90% of 300

10. How much will a $25 item cost you if there is 5% sales tax?
- Ⓐ $1.25
- Ⓑ $23.75
- Ⓒ $27.50
- Ⓓ $26.25

11. What decimal is equivalent to 37%?
- Ⓐ 37.0
- Ⓑ 3.7
- Ⓒ 0.37
- Ⓓ 0.037

12. 12% of what you spend with a special credit card is given back to you. If you spend $375.00, then how much money will you get back?
- Ⓐ $45.00
- Ⓑ $31.25
- Ⓒ $4.26
- Ⓓ $426.14

13. If 45% of a number is 145, then what is 70% of the number?
- Ⓐ 225.56
- Ⓑ 210
- Ⓒ 181.25
- Ⓓ 101.5

14. 30% of the desks in Hadley Middle School are made out of metal. How many metal desks are there if the school has 4,500 desks total?
- Ⓐ 3,150
- Ⓑ 150
- Ⓒ 1,500
- Ⓓ 1,350

15. Marcus left his waitress a 20% tip of $4.80. How much was his meal?
- Ⓐ $19.20
- Ⓑ $26.50
- Ⓒ $24.00
- Ⓓ $8.64

16. If 85% of a number is 555.9, then what percentage of the number is 124?
- Ⓐ 18.96%
- Ⓑ 22.31%
- Ⓒ 19.40%
- Ⓓ 17.89%

17. Which fraction is equivalent to 88%?
- Ⓐ $\frac{88}{1,000}$
- Ⓑ $\frac{264}{300}$
- Ⓒ $\frac{88}{1}$
- Ⓓ $\frac{348}{400}$

18. Nicholas got 70% of the way through a 150-question test. How many questions did he finish?
- Ⓐ 21
- Ⓑ 96
- Ⓒ 105
- Ⓓ 124

Integers

Answer the questions below.

1. −3 + 2 =
Ⓐ 5
Ⓑ −5
Ⓒ 1
Ⓓ −1

2. 7 − −4 =
Ⓐ 11
Ⓑ −11
Ⓒ 3
Ⓓ −3

3. −40 − −23 =
Ⓐ 17
Ⓑ −17
Ⓒ −63
Ⓓ 63

4. It was −3 degrees outside one winter night. The temperature went up 9 degrees the next day. What was the temperature during the day?
Ⓐ −12 degrees
Ⓑ 9 degrees
Ⓒ 6 degrees
Ⓓ −3 degrees

5. June had 8 French fries. Her friend Joseph wasn't hungry anymore and gave her 6 of his leftover fries. If June eats 9 fries altogether, then how many are left over?
Ⓐ 5
Ⓑ 7
Ⓒ 11
Ⓓ 23

6. If eleven birds were in a tree and seven of them left, then how many birds are still in the tree?
Ⓐ 3
Ⓑ 4
Ⓒ 6
Ⓓ 7

7. 127 − 252 =
Ⓐ −125
Ⓑ 125
Ⓒ −25
Ⓓ −379

8. 17 + y = 12, when y = ?
Ⓐ −29
Ⓑ 29
Ⓒ 5
Ⓓ −5

9. −7 × 5 =
Ⓐ 35
Ⓑ −2
Ⓒ −35
Ⓓ $-\dfrac{7}{5}$

10. 45 ÷ −9 =
Ⓐ 5
Ⓑ 405
Ⓒ −405
Ⓓ −5

11. −12 × −7 =
Ⓐ −84
Ⓑ 84
Ⓒ $\dfrac{12}{7}$
Ⓓ $-\dfrac{12}{7}$

12. $\dfrac{-125}{-5}$ =
Ⓐ 625
Ⓑ −25
Ⓒ −625
Ⓓ 25

Section 5: Algebra and Functions
Algebraic Equations

Solve for the variable.

1. $24 + x = 39$
- (A) 5
- (B) 63
- (C) 15
- (D) 53

2. $\dfrac{18}{z} = 3$
- (A) 6
- (B) 4
- (C) 9
- (D) 3

3. $19 = t - 13$
- (A) −6
- (B) 6
- (C) 22
- (D) 32

4. $\dfrac{p}{12} = -4$
- (A) −48
- (B) 3
- (C) 48
- (D) −3

5. $13\,j = 169$
- (A) 19
- (B) 17
- (C) 13
- (D) 9

6. $46 = 23 - s$
- (A) −69
- (B) 23
- (C) 69
- (D) −23

7. Jeremy wants to split his cake among him and his friends. If he has 20 pieces of cake and each person gets 5 pieces, then how many friends does he share it with?
- (A) 3
- (B) 4
- (C) 5
- (D) 6

8. A teacher divided candy among her 9 students evenly. Each student got 4 pieces and the teacher had 3 left over. How many pieces of candy were there in total?
- (A) 39
- (B) 36
- (C) 30
- (D) 27

9. Margaret bought 7 boxes each containing the same number of bananas. If she had 63 bananas in all, then how many bananas are in each box?
- (A) 6
- (B) 7
- (C) 8
- (D) 9

10. Jean is $\dfrac{1}{3}$ her brother's age plus 4. How old is Jean's brother if Jean is 12?
- (A) 42
- (B) 24
- (C) 12
- (D) 8

11. $59\,x = 649$
- (A) 21
- (B) 13
- (C) 11
- (D) 8

12. Eddy made $\dfrac{2}{5}$ more money than Heidi at the bake sale. If Heidi made $25, how much more did Eddy make?
- (A) $35
- (B) $15
- (C) $30
- (D) $10

Rates

Answer the questions below.

1. It takes a machine 24 minutes to fill 400 bottles with milk. At this rate, how long will it take to fill 1,000 bottles?
Ⓐ 36 minutes
Ⓑ 48 minutes
Ⓒ 60 minutes
Ⓓ 72 minutes

2. A small car can drive 35 miles on 1 gallon of gas. How many gallons would be needed to drive 175 miles?
Ⓐ 3
Ⓑ 5
Ⓒ 9
Ⓓ 13

3. Trish has 10 cars that she needs to wash in 45 minutes. What is the minimum rate she needs to wash at in order to finish in time?
Ⓐ 1.5 minutes per car
Ⓑ 3.5 minutes per car
Ⓒ 4.0 minutes per car
Ⓓ 4.5 minutes per car

4. Which of the following rates is a unit rate?
Ⓐ 10 hours / 1 yard
Ⓑ 1 gallon / 3 days
Ⓒ 9 pounds / 5 feet
Ⓓ 3 years / 2 years

5. An apple tree is found to have 1 worm per 7 apples. How many apples are on the tree if there are 11 worms?
Ⓐ 65
Ⓑ 77
Ⓒ 11
Ⓓ 1.6

6. Which of the following is a rate?
Ⓐ $\frac{9}{17}$
Ⓑ $\frac{5}{1}$
Ⓒ 5 puppies per 2 dogs
Ⓓ 6 years per 1

7. Washing machines at a laundromat can wash 10 pounds of clothes per hour. How many pounds of clothes would you have if it took 4.5 hours to wash them?
Ⓐ 45 pounds
Ⓑ 35 pounds
Ⓒ 55 pounds
Ⓓ 4.5 pounds

8. It takes 5 buckets of sand per 2 sand castles. What is the unit rate?
Ⓐ 5 buckets of sand / 2 sand castles
Ⓑ 1 bucket of sand / 0.4 sand castles
Ⓒ 2.5 buckets / 1 sand castle
Ⓓ 10 buckets of sand / 4 sand castles

Patterns and Functions

Answer the questions below.

1. Which number comes next in the pattern below?

    8, 15, 22, 29, __

Ⓐ 31
Ⓑ 33
Ⓒ 36
Ⓓ 37

2. What is the rule for the pattern below?

    7, 14, 28, 56

Ⓐ add 7
Ⓑ add 28
Ⓒ divide by 2
Ⓓ multiply by 2

3. Which function represents the data in the following table?

Ⓐ $y = x + 5$
Ⓑ $y = x + 8$
Ⓒ $y = 2x + 2$
Ⓓ $y = \dfrac{x - 2}{2}$

x	3	4	5	6
y	8	10	12	14

4. What number is missing from the pattern below?

    36, 31, __, 21, 16

Ⓐ 26
Ⓑ 29
Ⓒ 23
Ⓓ 28

5. Which number table would be made by the function $y = \dfrac{1}{3} x + 1$?

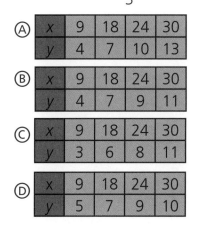

Ⓐ

x	9	18	24	30
y	4	7	10	13

Ⓑ

x	9	18	24	30
y	4	7	9	11

Ⓒ

x	9	18	24	30
y	3	6	8	11

Ⓓ

x	9	18	24	30
y	5	7	9	10

6. Which number sequence is made by using the rule *divide by 3*?

Ⓐ 81, 27, 19, 6
Ⓑ 540, 180, 60, 20
Ⓒ 1, 3, 9, 27
Ⓓ 18, 15, 12, 9

7. Which number would complete the following table?

Ⓐ 20
Ⓑ 21
Ⓒ 22
Ⓓ 23

x	3	6	8	11
y	8	17	?	32

8. Which number completes the pattern below?

    93, 76, __, 42, 25?

Ⓐ 69
Ⓑ 63
Ⓒ 61
Ⓓ 59

Coordinates

Use the graph below to answer the questions.

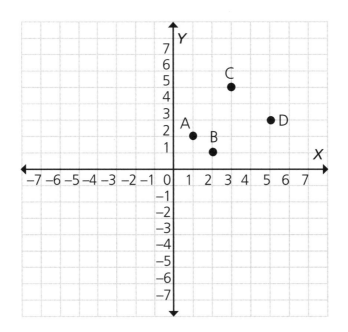

1. Which ordered pair
represents point C?
Ⓐ (1,2)
Ⓑ (2,1)
Ⓒ (3,5)
Ⓓ (5,3)

2. Which of the following
points is represented by the
ordered pair (2,1)?
Ⓐ Point A
Ⓑ Point B
Ⓒ Point C
Ⓓ Point D

3. Which ordered pair
represents point D?
Ⓐ (1,2)
Ⓑ (2,1)
Ⓒ (3,5)
Ⓓ (5,3)

4. Which of the following
points is represented by the
ordered pair (1,2)?
Ⓐ Point A
Ⓑ Point B
Ⓒ Point C
Ⓓ Point D

5. Which ordered pair would be
found in quadrant II of a
graph?
Ⓐ (−3,5)
Ⓑ (2,−6)
Ⓒ (4,2)
Ⓓ (−1,6)

6. Which ordered pair would
be found in quadrant IV of a
graph?
Ⓐ (5,8)
Ⓑ (3,−4)
Ⓒ (−7,3)
Ⓓ (−2,−4)

Evaluating Expressions

Answer the questions below.

1. Which is the proper expression to represent "*a* more than 17"?
- Ⓐ $a - 17$
- Ⓑ $17 - a$
- Ⓒ $17 + a$
- Ⓓ $17\,a$

2. Evaluate $c \times 7$, when $c = 3$?
- Ⓐ $\frac{3}{7}$
- Ⓑ 14
- Ⓒ 19
- Ⓓ 21

3. Terry threw a ball *h* yards. Jill threw a ball 23 yards less than Terry. Which expression represents how far Jill threw the ball?
- Ⓐ $h - 23$
- Ⓑ $23 - h$
- Ⓒ $h + 23$
- Ⓓ $23 + h$

4. Which expression shows "17 divided by *f*"?
- Ⓐ $17 + f$
- Ⓑ $17 \div f$
- Ⓒ $f \div 17$
- Ⓓ $17 - f$

5. Evaluate $r \div 6$, when $r = 42$.
- Ⓐ 4
- Ⓑ 6
- Ⓒ 7
- Ⓓ 42

6. Evaluate $6q + 12$, when $q = 5$.
- Ⓐ 23
- Ⓑ 37
- Ⓒ 42
- Ⓓ 90

Solve for the variable.

7. $27 + a = 39$
- Ⓐ 11
- Ⓑ 12
- Ⓒ 13
- Ⓓ 14

8. $\frac{32}{x} = 4$
- Ⓐ 6
- Ⓑ 7
- Ⓒ 8
- Ⓓ 9

9. $\frac{112}{y} = 14$
- Ⓐ 3
- Ⓑ 6
- Ⓒ 8
- Ⓓ 16

10. $42 = 14h$
- Ⓐ 1
- Ⓑ 2
- Ⓒ 3
- Ⓓ 4

11. $b - 93 = 156$
- Ⓐ 149
- Ⓑ 249
- Ⓒ 148
- Ⓓ 63

12. $14 + c = 27$
- Ⓐ 13
- Ⓑ 31
- Ⓒ 11
- Ⓓ 9

Order of Operations

Answer the questions below.

1. $3 + 2 \times 4 =$
- Ⓐ 20
- Ⓑ 24
- Ⓒ 11
- Ⓓ 14

2. $18 \div 2 + 4 \times 3 =$
- Ⓐ 21
- Ⓑ 39
- Ⓒ 9
- Ⓓ 1

3. $(3 + 7) \times 5 - 1 =$
- Ⓐ 37
- Ⓑ 40
- Ⓒ 48
- Ⓓ 49

4. $\dfrac{6 + 10}{2} - 3 =$
- Ⓐ 10
- Ⓑ 5
- Ⓒ 8
- Ⓓ 6.5

5. Joey bought 5 erasers for $0.25 each and 3 pencils for $0.75 each. How much did he pay in total?
- Ⓐ $3.50
- Ⓑ $4.50
- Ⓒ $5.00
- Ⓓ $5.25

6. Geraldine has 5 photo books of 30 photos each. If 100 of the photos have her in them, then how many photos do **not** have Geraldine in them?
- Ⓐ 100
- Ⓑ 70
- Ⓒ 50
- Ⓓ 30

7. $5 \times (7 + 5) \div 4 =$
- Ⓐ 10
- Ⓑ 15
- Ⓒ 25
- Ⓓ 36.25

8. $3(19 - 12) + 5 \times 2 =$
- Ⓐ 31
- Ⓑ 55
- Ⓒ 72
- Ⓓ 100

9. $26 \div 2 - 3 \times 4 =$
- Ⓐ 64
- Ⓑ 25
- Ⓒ 1
- Ⓓ 40

10. $7(26 - 14) + 6 \times 5 =$
- Ⓐ 95
- Ⓑ 390
- Ⓒ 870
- Ⓓ 114

Geometric Formulas

Answer the questions below.

1. Which is the correct formula for the perimeter of a rectangle?
- (A) $P = 2(l + w)$
- (B) $P = 2lw$
- (C) $P = l + w$
- (D) $P = lwh$

2. Which is the correct formula for the circumference of a circle?
- (A) $C = \pi 4r^2$
- (B) $C = \pi d$
- (C) $C = 2\pi d$
- (D) $C = 2\pi r^2$

3. Which is the correct formula for the area of a triangle?
- (A) $A = 2bh$
- (B) $A = \frac{1}{2}\frac{b}{h}$
- (C) $A = bh$
- (D) $A = \frac{1}{2}bh$

4. Which is the correct formula for the area of a circle?
- (A) $A = 2\pi r$
- (B) $A = \pi r^2$
- (C) $A = \pi d^2$
- (D) $A = 2\pi r^2$

5. Which is the correct formula for the area of a trapezoid?
- (A) $A = b_1 h + b_2 h$
- (B) $A = 2h(b_1 + b_2)$
- (C) $A = \frac{1}{2}h(b_1 + b_2)$
- (D) $A = 2h + b_1 + b_2$

6. Which is the correct formula for the area of a square?
- (A) $A = 2(lw)$
- (B) $A = l + w$
- (C) $A = \frac{1}{2}lw$
- (D) $A = lw$

7. Which of the following formulas would give you the length of a rectangle with a width of 30 cm and a perimeter of 100 cm?
- (A) $100 = 60 + l$
- (B) $100 = 60 + 2l$
- (C) $60 = 100 + l$
- (D) $100 = 30l$

8. Which expression represents the blue area of the picture below in terms of z?
- (A) $64 + z^2$
- (B) $64 - 2z$
- (C) $64 - z^2$
- (D) $z^2 - 64$

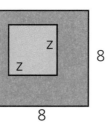

Section 6: Measurement and Geometry
Rays, Lines, and Planes

Use the figure below to answer questions 1–3.

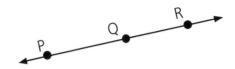

1. Which of the following is a ray?
- Ⓐ $\overleftrightarrow{PR}$
- Ⓑ $\overrightarrow{QR}$
- Ⓒ $\overline{PQ}$
- Ⓓ $\overline{PR}$

2. Which of the following is a line segment?
- Ⓐ $\overleftrightarrow{QR}$
- Ⓑ $\overrightarrow{QP}$
- Ⓒ $\overline{PR}$
- Ⓓ $\overrightarrow{RP}$

3. Which of the following is a line?
- Ⓐ $\overleftrightarrow{PR}$
- Ⓑ $\overrightarrow{PQ}$
- Ⓒ $\overline{PR}$
- Ⓓ $\overrightarrow{QR}$

Identify the type of lines.

4.

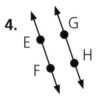

- Ⓐ perpendicular
- Ⓑ skew
- Ⓒ parallel
- Ⓓ intersecting

5.

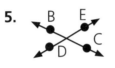

- Ⓐ perpendicular
- Ⓑ skew
- Ⓒ parallel
- Ⓓ intersecting

6.

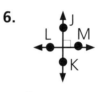

- Ⓐ perpendicular
- Ⓑ skew
- Ⓒ parallel
- Ⓓ intersecting

7. Two lines that are **not** in the same plane are an example of _____ lines.
- Ⓐ perpendicular
- Ⓑ skew
- Ⓒ parallel
- Ⓓ intersecting

8. Which of the following is a possible name for the figure below?

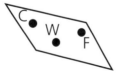

- Ⓐ Plane C
- Ⓑ Point W
- Ⓒ $\overleftrightarrow{WF}$
- Ⓓ Plane CWF

9. Which of the following is a possible name for the figure below?

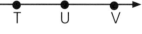

- Ⓐ Plane U
- Ⓑ $\overleftrightarrow{TV}$
- Ⓒ Plane TUV
- Ⓓ Point U

Angles

Answer the questions below.

1. One angle in a right triangle is 37 degrees. What is the measure of the other non-right angle?
   Ⓐ 53 degrees
   Ⓑ 63 degrees
   Ⓒ 233 degrees
   Ⓓ 243 degrees

2. Which angle is supplementary to 76 degrees?
   Ⓐ 14 degrees
   Ⓑ 24 degrees
   Ⓒ 104 degrees
   Ⓓ 284 degrees

3. Which angle is complementary to 54 degrees?
   Ⓐ 26 degrees
   Ⓑ 36 degrees
   Ⓒ 126 degrees
   Ⓓ 306 degrees

4. Which of the following angles is an obtuse angle?
   Ⓐ 37 degrees
   Ⓑ 45 degrees
   Ⓒ 75 degrees
   Ⓓ 97 degrees

5. What kind of angle is 180 degrees?
   Ⓐ obtuse
   Ⓑ straight
   Ⓒ right
   Ⓓ acute

6. Which angle is supplementary to 27 degrees?
   Ⓐ 153 degrees
   Ⓑ 63 degrees
   Ⓒ 207 degrees
   Ⓓ 117 degrees

Use the figure below to answer questions 7–9.

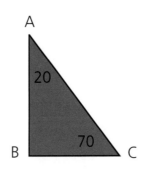

7. What type of angle is ∠ABC?
   Ⓐ right
   Ⓑ obtuse
   Ⓒ acute
   Ⓓ straight

8. What type of angle is ∠BAC?
   Ⓐ right
   Ⓑ obtuse
   Ⓒ acute
   Ⓓ straight

9. Which angle is supplementary to ∠ACB?
   Ⓐ 20
   Ⓑ 160
   Ⓒ 70
   Ⓓ 110

Plane Figures

Identify the plane figures.

1.

Ⓐ rhombus
Ⓑ rectangle
Ⓒ trapezoid
Ⓓ parallelogram

2.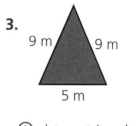

Ⓐ rhombus
Ⓑ parallelogram
Ⓒ rectangle
Ⓓ trapezoid

3.

9 m   9 m

5 m

Ⓐ obtuse triangle
Ⓑ isosceles triangle
Ⓒ scalene triangle
Ⓓ equilateral triangle

4.

Ⓐ obtuse triangle
Ⓑ isosceles triangle
Ⓒ scalene triangle
Ⓓ equilateral triangle

5.

4 ft   4 ft

4 ft

Ⓐ obtuse triangle
Ⓑ equilateral triangle
Ⓒ right triangle
Ⓓ isosceles triangle

6.

Ⓐ equilateral triangle
Ⓑ scalene triangle
Ⓒ acute triangle
Ⓓ right triangle

Use the figure below to answer questions 7–9.

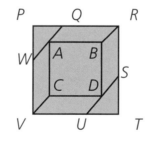

7. Which of the following is a hexagon?
Ⓐ PWVCAQ
Ⓑ WQRBDCV
Ⓒ WVUSRQ
Ⓓ ABRSDT

8. Which of the following is a triangle?
Ⓐ PWR
Ⓑ SUT
Ⓒ ABR
Ⓓ ADR

9. Which of the following is a parallelogram?
Ⓐ CDUV
Ⓑ PWQR
Ⓒ WVUD
Ⓓ ABSD

Measurements

Answer the questions below.

1. Cathy wants to measure how big her garden is. What would be the most appropriate unit of measure to use?
   - Ⓐ inches
   - Ⓑ feet
   - Ⓒ ounces
   - Ⓓ miles

2. Which of the following is the largest measurement?
   - Ⓐ 1 yd
   - Ⓑ 2.5 ft
   - Ⓒ 50 cm
   - Ⓓ 37 in

3. Which of the following is the smallest measurement?
   - Ⓐ 6 fl oz
   - Ⓑ 2 c
   - Ⓒ 1 pt
   - Ⓓ 2 qt

4. What unit would you use to get the most accurate measurement of the length of a carrot?
   - Ⓐ feet
   - Ⓑ yards
   - Ⓒ inches
   - Ⓓ millimeters

5. Which of the following is the smallest measurement?
   - Ⓐ 137 seconds
   - Ⓑ 2.5 hours
   - Ⓒ 3 minutes
   - Ⓓ 4 days

6. Which of the following is the most precise unit of measure?
   - Ⓐ grams
   - Ⓑ ounces
   - Ⓒ pounds
   - Ⓓ kilograms

7. What would be the most appropriate unit to measure the distance between two cities?
   - Ⓐ feet
   - Ⓑ grams
   - Ⓒ miles
   - Ⓓ inches

8. Which of the following measurements is the most precise?
   - Ⓐ 1 hour
   - Ⓑ 59 minutes
   - Ⓒ 3,550 seconds
   - Ⓓ 0.04 days

Units of Measurement

Answer the questions below.

1. How many inches are in 3.5 feet?
Ⓐ 21
Ⓑ 36
Ⓒ 42
Ⓓ 48

2. Kenny's birthday is in $16\frac{1}{2}$ weeks. How many days is it until Kenny's birthday?
Ⓐ 108.5
Ⓑ 112.5
Ⓒ 115.5
Ⓓ 122.5

3. How many ounces are in $2\frac{3}{4}$ pounds?
Ⓐ 44
Ⓑ 38.5
Ⓒ 33
Ⓓ 22

4. Jessica measures a piece of paper to be 11 inches. How many centimeters is the piece of paper?
Ⓐ 4.3
Ⓑ 7.1
Ⓒ 16.9
Ⓓ 27.9

Convert to the given unit.

5. 3 kg = _____ g
Ⓐ 300
Ⓑ 30
Ⓒ 0.003
Ⓓ 3,000

6. 2.5 cL = _____ mL
Ⓐ 25
Ⓑ 0.25
Ⓒ 250
Ⓓ 0.025

7. 220 min = _____ hr
Ⓐ $9\frac{1}{6}$
Ⓑ $5\frac{1}{2}$
Ⓒ 13,200
Ⓓ $3\frac{2}{3}$

8. 22 fl oz = _____ c
Ⓐ 176
Ⓑ $3\frac{2}{3}$
Ⓒ $2\frac{3}{4}$
Ⓓ $1\frac{3}{8}$

9. 26 cm = _____ km
Ⓐ 260
Ⓑ 0.00026
Ⓒ 2.6
Ⓓ 0.0026

10. 3.5 mi = _____ ft
Ⓐ 18,480
Ⓑ 18,410
Ⓒ 18,980
Ⓓ 14,910

11. 6.5 cm = _____ in
- (A) 16.51
- (B) 2.56
- (C) 1.84
- (D) 10.01

12. 18 fl oz = _____ p
- (A) 1.5
- (B) 0.75
- (C) 1.125
- (D) 0.5625

13. 3,257 s = _____ hr
- (A) 54.28
- (B) 0.9
- (C) 27.14
- (D) 2.26

14. 1.5 kg = _____ mg
- (A) 1,500
- (B) 150,000
- (C) 1,500,000
- (D) 15,000,000

15. 3.5 mi = _____ km
- (A) 6.3
- (B) 2.19
- (C) 1.94
- (D) 5.6

16. 14 p = _____ gal
- (A) 1.75
- (B) 3.5
- (C) 0.875
- (D) 7

17. 4 q = _____ L
- (A) 1.89
- (B) 3.78
- (C) 7.56
- (D) 2

18. 4.7 lb = _____ kg
- (A) 10.34
- (B) 0.214
- (C) 2.14
- (D) 1.034

Add or subtract the two measurements.

19. 2.5 lb + 12 oz =
- (A) 3.4 lb
- (B) 3 lb 4 oz
- (C) 3 lb 1 oz
- (D) 3.1 lb

20. 2.25 q − 4 c =
- (A) 5 c
- (B) 0.5 c
- (C) 1.75 q
- (D) 2 q

21. 4 gal − 8 p =
- (A) 12 p
- (B) 4 p
- (C) 3 gal
- (D) .25 gal

22. 12 q − 1.5 gal =
- (A) 3 gal
- (B) 10.5 gal
- (C) 18 q
- (D) 6 q

Perimeter and Circumference

Answer the questions below.

1. What is the circumference of a circle that has a diameter of 12 yards?
- Ⓐ 18.8 yards
- Ⓑ 37.7 yards
- Ⓒ 75.4 yards
- Ⓓ 113 yards

2. If a circle has a circumference of 25 feet, then what is the radius of the circle?
- Ⓐ 2
- Ⓑ 4
- Ⓒ 8
- Ⓓ 10

3. The figure below has a perimeter of 108 yd. What is the measurement of side a?
- Ⓐ 27 yd.
- Ⓑ 28 yd.
- Ⓒ 29 yd.
- Ⓓ 30 yd.

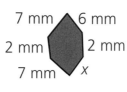

16 yd. a 26 yd. 29 yd. 7 yd.

4. What is the perimeter of the figure?
- Ⓐ 43 yd.
- Ⓑ 420 yd.
- Ⓒ 86 yd.
- Ⓓ 210 yd.

15 yd. 28 yd.

5. Pi can be found by _____.
- Ⓐ dividing the circumference of a circle by its diameter
- Ⓑ dividing the area of a circle by its radius
- Ⓒ dividing the circumference of a circle by its radius
- Ⓓ dividing the area of a circle by its diameter

6. What is the perimeter of the figure?
- Ⓐ 6.79 m
- Ⓑ 16 m
- Ⓒ 8 m
- Ⓓ 13.57 m

5.56 m 3.8 m 4.21 m

7. The figure below has a perimeter of 29 mm. What is the measurement of side x?
- Ⓐ 5 mm
- Ⓑ 6 mm
- Ⓒ 7 mm
- Ⓓ 8 mm

7 mm 6 mm 2 mm 2 mm 7 mm x

8. What is the circumference of the circle?
- Ⓐ 23.9 cm
- Ⓑ 47.7 cm
- Ⓒ 60.8 cm
- Ⓓ 181.4 m

7.6 cm

Area

Answer the questions below.

1. What is the area of a rectangular field that has a length of 30 yards and a width of 15 yards?
Ⓐ 90 yd.²
Ⓑ 450 yd.²
Ⓒ 45 yd.²
Ⓓ 900 yd.²

2. A pizza pie has an 18-inch diameter. What is the area of the pie?
Ⓐ 1,017.7 in.²
Ⓑ 113.1 in.²
Ⓒ 28.3 in.²
Ⓓ 254.4 in.²

3. What is the diameter of a circle that has an area of 75 m²?
Ⓐ 23.9 m
Ⓑ 9.8 m
Ⓒ 4.9 m
Ⓓ 3.7 m

4. If a rectangle has an area of 40 inches² and a width of 2 inches, then what is the length of the rectangle?
Ⓐ 20 in.
Ⓑ 10 in.
Ⓒ 30 in.
Ⓓ 4 in.

Calculate the area of each shape.

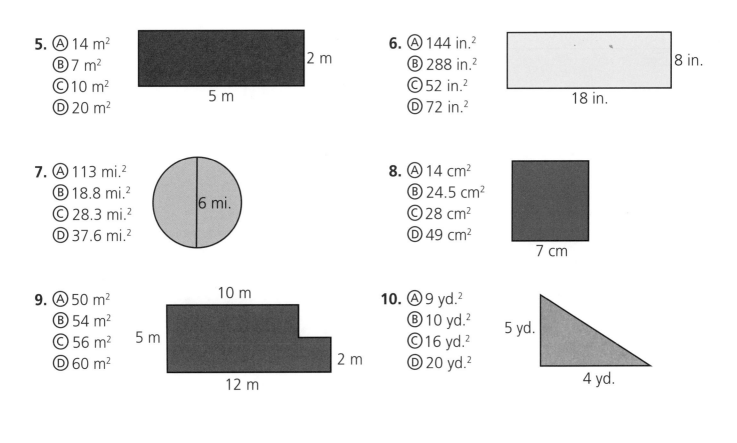

5. Ⓐ 14 m²
Ⓑ 7 m²
Ⓒ 10 m²
Ⓓ 20 m²

2 m
5 m

6. Ⓐ 144 in.²
Ⓑ 288 in.²
Ⓒ 52 in.²
Ⓓ 72 in.²

8 in.
18 in.

7. Ⓐ 113 mi.²
Ⓑ 18.8 mi.²
Ⓒ 28.3 mi.²
Ⓓ 37.6 mi.²

6 mi.

8. Ⓐ 14 cm²
Ⓑ 24.5 cm²
Ⓒ 28 cm²
Ⓓ 49 cm²

7 cm

9. Ⓐ 50 m²
Ⓑ 54 m²
Ⓒ 56 m²
Ⓓ 60 m²

10 m
5 m
2 m
12 m

10. Ⓐ 9 yd.²
Ⓑ 10 yd.²
Ⓒ 16 yd.²
Ⓓ 20 yd.²

5 yd.
4 yd.

Solid Figures

Use the figures below to answer questions 1–4.

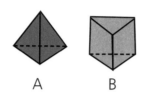

A   B   C   D

1. Which of the shapes is a rectangular prism?
- Ⓐ A
- Ⓑ B
- Ⓒ C
- Ⓓ D

2. Which of the shapes is a triangular pyramid?
- Ⓐ A
- Ⓑ B
- Ⓒ C
- Ⓓ D

3. Which of the shapes is a rectangular pyramid?
- Ⓐ A
- Ⓑ B
- Ⓒ C
- Ⓓ D

4. Which of the shapes is a triangular prism?
- Ⓐ A
- Ⓑ B
- Ⓒ C
- Ⓓ D

Determine the shape of the figure with the views shown.

5.

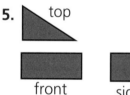

top

front   side

- Ⓐ rectangular prism
- Ⓑ triangular pyramid
- Ⓒ triangle
- Ⓓ triangular prism

6.

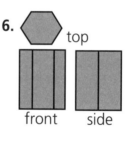

top

front   side

- Ⓐ octagonal prism
- Ⓑ octagonal pyramid
- Ⓒ hexagonal prism
- Ⓓ hexagonal pyramid

7.

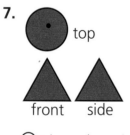

top

front   side

- Ⓐ triangular prism
- Ⓑ cone
- Ⓒ cylinder
- Ⓓ circular prism

8.

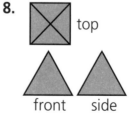

top

front   side

- Ⓐ square pyramid
- Ⓑ triangular prism
- Ⓒ triangular pyramid
- Ⓓ pentagonal pyramid

Transformations

Answer the questions below.

1. What type of transformation has occurred when a shape is moved up 5 units?
- Ⓐ reflection
- Ⓑ vertical translation
- Ⓒ horizontal translation
- Ⓓ rotation

2. What type of transformation has occurred when the point (3,2) becomes (0,2)?
- Ⓐ reflection
- Ⓑ vertical translation
- Ⓒ horizontal translation
- Ⓓ rotation

Identify the transformation that has occurred to the gray shape.

3.

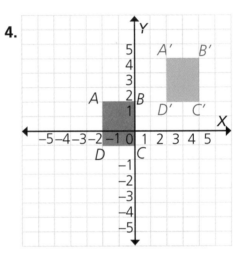

- Ⓐ rotated 90 degrees counterclockwise around (0,0)
- Ⓑ translated 1 unit down
- Ⓒ reflected over the x-axis
- Ⓓ reflected over the y-axis

4.

- Ⓐ reflected over the y-axis
- Ⓑ rotated 180 degrees clockwise around (1,3)
- Ⓒ translated 3 units right and 4 up
- Ⓓ translated 4 units right and 3 up

5.

- Ⓐ rotated 90 degrees clockwise around (0,0)
- Ⓑ reflected over the x-axis
- Ⓒ translated down 4 units
- Ⓓ rotated 180 degrees around (0,0)

Volume

Find the volume of the figures below.

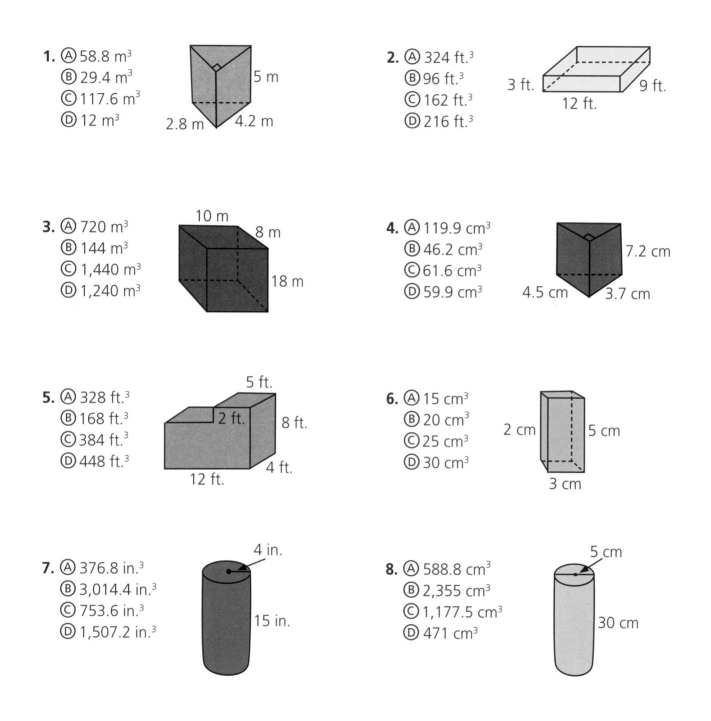

1. (A) 58.8 m³
(B) 29.4 m³
(C) 117.6 m³
(D) 12 m³

5 m
2.8 m   4.2 m

2. (A) 324 ft.³
(B) 96 ft.³
(C) 162 ft.³
(D) 216 ft.³

3 ft.   9 ft.
12 ft.

3. (A) 720 m³
(B) 144 m³
(C) 1,440 m³
(D) 1,240 m³

10 m
8 m
18 m

4. (A) 119.9 cm³
(B) 46.2 cm³
(C) 61.6 cm³
(D) 59.9 cm³

7.2 cm
4.5 cm   3.7 cm

5. (A) 328 ft.³
(B) 168 ft.³
(C) 384 ft.³
(D) 448 ft.³

5 ft.
2 ft.   8 ft.
4 ft.
12 ft.

6. (A) 15 cm³
(B) 20 cm³
(C) 25 cm³
(D) 30 cm³

2 cm   5 cm
3 cm

7. (A) 376.8 in.³
(B) 3,014.4 in.³
(C) 753.6 in.³
(D) 1,507.2 in.³

4 in.
15 in.

8. (A) 588.8 cm³
(B) 2,355 cm³
(C) 1,177.5 cm³
(D) 471 cm³

5 cm
30 cm

Section 7: Statistics, Data Analysis, and Probability

Central Tendency

Answer the questions below.

1. What is the mean of the data set below?

   4, 7, 9, 11, 3

   Ⓐ 6.8
   Ⓑ 9
   Ⓒ 8.5
   Ⓓ no answer

2. What is the median of the data set below?

   12, 21, 5, 21, 18

   Ⓐ 15.4
   Ⓑ 21
   Ⓒ 18
   Ⓓ no answer

3. The following data set has a mean of 45: 36, 39, *x*, 49, 53. What is the value of *x*?

   Ⓐ 45
   Ⓑ 37
   Ⓒ 3
   Ⓓ 48

4. Gregory took 5 tests throughout the year. He scored 93, 84, 97, 89, and 93. What is the mean of Gregory's test scores?

   Ⓐ 93
   Ⓑ 91.2
   Ⓒ 92.2
   Ⓓ no answer

5. What is the mode of the data set below?

   24, 41, 27, 26, 52, 11

   Ⓐ 30.2
   Ⓑ 36.2
   Ⓒ 46.2
   Ⓓ no answer

6. Lauryn drove to visit her friend four times this month. It took her an average of 1.4 hours to drive there. If her first three trips took her 1.7 hours, 1.2 hours, and 1.6 hours, then how long did her last trip take?

   Ⓐ 1.1 hours
   Ⓑ 1.4 hours
   Ⓒ 1.8 hours
   Ⓓ 2.5 hours

Use the table below to answer questions 7–8.

Game	1	2	3	4	5	6	7	8
Points Scored	10	13	10	17	18	12	20	24

7. What is the mean of the points scored for all of the games?

   Ⓐ 17.5
   Ⓑ 15.5
   Ⓒ 62
   Ⓓ 15

8. What is the mode of the points scored for all of the games?

   Ⓐ 10
   Ⓑ 15.5
   Ⓒ 15
   Ⓓ 12.5

Sampling

Answer the questions below.

1. Mindy wants to find out the most popular baseball team at a game between the home team and the visiting team. Which method would give Mindy the most accurate results?
   (A) Survey everyone with sunglasses.
   (B) Survey the cheerleaders for the visiting team.
   (C) Survey a group of people waiting in line to buy food.
   (D) Survey people who are sitting in the home team's bleachers.

2. Ling wants to find out about the study habits of teenagers in her state. If she puts an ad in newspapers throughout the state asking for teenagers to respond to her survey, what method of sampling is she using?
   (A) self-selected sampling
   (B) convenience sampling
   (C) systematic sampling
   (D) random sampling

3. Ryan is taking a survey on favorite TV shows of people in his state. If he stands on the same corner in his town every day for three days, what method of sampling is he using?
   (A) self-selected sampling
   (B) convenience sampling
   (C) systematic sampling
   (D) random sampling

4. Kara thinks that the school buses in her district need to be updated. To see if riders on all the buses agree, she obtains a list of all the students who take the bus and then randomly chooses names of people to interview. What method of sampling is Kara using?
   (A) self-selected sampling
   (B) convenience sampling
   (C) systematic sampling
   (D) random sampling

5. Suppose you want to find out how many hours a day teenagers in your county spend doing homework and studying. What is the **best** way to get accurate, unbiased results?
   (A) Interview every fifth student on class rosters from the local schools.
   (B) Select teenagers at random from a list of county residents.
   (C) Post signs in the local schools asking teenagers to respond.
   (D) Go to the library and ask the teenagers you find there.

6. Suppose you want to find out the most popular fiction genre in your town. What is the **best** way to get accurate, unbiased results?
   (A) Stand in the horror section of your school library and ask the students who come by.
   (B) Stand outside a bookstore and ask every person who walks into the store.
   (C) Post an ad on a romance novel website and ask for volunteers.
   (D) Randomly call people from your town's phone book and ask them their opinion.

Graphs

Answer the questions below.

1. What type of graph would **best** be used to show how Janet spent her Christmas money?
Ⓐ line graph
Ⓑ bar graph
Ⓒ circle graph
Ⓓ stem-and-leaf graph

2. Which type of graph would be **best** used to show the change in a stock price over time?
Ⓐ line graph
Ⓑ bar graph
Ⓒ circle graph
Ⓓ stem-and-leaf graph

3. Which type of graph would **best** be used to compare the different weights of seven elephants?
Ⓐ line graph
Ⓑ bar graph
Ⓒ circle graph
Ⓓ stem-and-leaf graph

4. Which type of graph would **best** be used to show how many customers come into a restaurant during each time interval?
Ⓐ histogram
Ⓑ line graph
Ⓒ box-and-whisker graph
Ⓓ stem-and-leaf graph

5. Which type of graph would **best** be used to show how widely distributed the different ages of a population are?
Ⓐ histogram
Ⓑ line graph
Ⓒ box-and-whisker graph
Ⓓ stem-and-leaf graph

6. What is the upper quartile of the graph below?

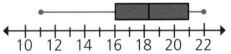

Ⓐ 16
Ⓑ 18
Ⓒ 21
Ⓓ 22

7. What is the median of the graph below?

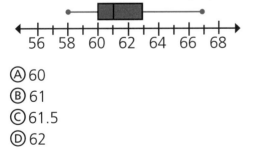

Ⓐ 60
Ⓑ 61
Ⓒ 61.5
Ⓓ 62

8. What is the lower quartile of the graph below?

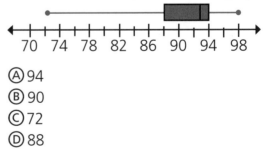

Ⓐ 94
Ⓑ 90
Ⓒ 72
Ⓓ 88

Circle Graphs

Use the graph below to answer the questions.

Money Raised at School Fair

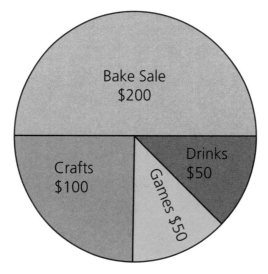

1. What percentage of the total money raised was raised from games?
   - (A) 14.3%
   - (B) 12.5%
   - (C) 25%
   - (D) 50%

2. What percentage of the total money raised was raised by means other than crafts?
   - (A) 75%
   - (B) 66.6%
   - (C) 50%
   - (D) 25%

3. How much more money was raised at the bake sale than the crafts and drinks combined?
   - (A) $100
   - (B) $75
   - (C) $50
   - (D) $25

4. If twice the amount of money was raised at the fair and the distributions stayed constant, then how much money would the crafts have made?
   - (A) $400
   - (B) $200
   - (C) $150
   - (D) $100

Interpreting Data

Use the chart below to answer the questions.

Company	Profit
I	$425,000
II	$350,000
III	$325,000
IV	$175,000
V	$150,000

1. Which of the following statements is true about the companies' profit?
Ⓐ Companies III and I made the same amount.
Ⓑ Company V made $25,000 less than IV.
Ⓒ All of the companies made over $250,000.
Ⓓ None of the companies made more than $300,000.

2. How much more profit did Company I make compared to Company III?
Ⓐ $75,000
Ⓑ $25,000
Ⓒ $100,000
Ⓓ $50,000

3. Which of the following combined profits for two companies are equal?
Ⓐ II + III and IV + V
Ⓑ II + V and III + IV
Ⓒ I + V and II + IV
Ⓓ III + V and I + IV

4. Which company made the most profit?
Ⓐ I
Ⓑ II
Ⓒ IV
Ⓓ V

Use the chart below to answer questions 5–6.

Lottery Year	Amount Won (millions of dollars)
1992	35
1993	31
1994	37
1995	44
1996	52
1997	46
1998	51
1999	55

5. Which statement about the amount of money won in the lottery is true?
Ⓐ More than 35 million was won every year.
Ⓑ The least amount won in a year is 31 million.
Ⓒ The most money was won in 1996.
Ⓓ The amount won in 1993 and 1994 is the same.

6. How much more money was won in 1997 than in 1993?
Ⓐ 20 million
Ⓑ 18 million
Ⓒ 16 million
Ⓓ 15 million

Probability

Answer the questions below.

1. If there is a 20% chance that an egg laid by a chicken is bad, then what is the chance of the egg being good?
- Ⓐ 30%
- Ⓑ 60%
- Ⓒ 75%
- Ⓓ 80%

2. Jack has a bag of twelve marbles. If seven of the marbles are red, then what is the probability that a marble picked at random will **not** be red?
- Ⓐ $\frac{7}{12}$
- Ⓑ $\frac{5}{12}$
- Ⓒ $\frac{5}{7}$
- Ⓓ $\frac{7}{5}$

3. What is the probability of rolling a 3 or a 4 on a die?
- Ⓐ $\frac{1}{6}$
- Ⓑ $\frac{1}{2}$
- Ⓒ $\frac{1}{3}$
- Ⓓ $\frac{2}{3}$

4. A coin is flipped two times. What is the probability that the coin landed on heads both times?
- Ⓐ $\frac{1}{4}$
- Ⓑ $\frac{1}{2}$
- Ⓒ $\frac{2}{3}$
- Ⓓ $\frac{3}{4}$

5. A computer company finds out that 3 out of every 28 of their computers are defective. If the company makes 336 in one week, then how many of them will probably be defective?
- Ⓐ 12
- Ⓑ 24
- Ⓒ 36
- Ⓓ 72

6. A machine chooses a number randomly between 1 and 5. What is the probability that the machine will choose an even number?
- Ⓐ $\frac{1}{2}$
- Ⓑ $\frac{2}{5}$
- Ⓒ $\frac{3}{5}$
- Ⓓ $\frac{1}{3}$

Use the figure below to answer questions 7–8.

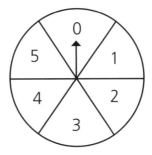

7. If the spinner is spun once, then what is the probability of it landing on a number greater than 1?

Ⓐ $\frac{2}{4}$

Ⓑ $\frac{4}{2}$

Ⓒ $\frac{5}{6}$

Ⓓ $\frac{2}{3}$

8. If the spinner is spun twice, then what is the probability of it landing on an odd number and then a number greater than 4?

Ⓐ $\frac{1}{12}$

Ⓑ $\frac{2}{3}$

Ⓒ $\frac{1}{3}$

Ⓓ $\frac{1}{10}$

Use the data from a spinner in the chart below to answer questions 9–10.

Red	Blue	Green	White	Pink	Yellow
卌 II	III	IIII	III	I	卌 III

9. What is the probability of the spinner landing on blue?

Ⓐ $\frac{1}{8}$

Ⓑ $\frac{1}{7}$

Ⓒ $\frac{1}{6}$

Ⓓ $\frac{1}{4}$

10. What is the probability of the spinner landing on white or yellow?

Ⓐ $\frac{5}{7}$

Ⓑ $\frac{5}{12}$

Ⓒ $\frac{10}{21}$

Ⓓ $\frac{7}{12}$

Section 8: Mathematical Reasoning
Choosing an Operation

Choose the operation that you would use to solve the problem.

1. Marc's soccer team has 7 points. The opposing team has 12 points. How many points does Marc's team need to tie the game?
- (A) addition
- (B) subtraction
- (C) multiplication
- (D) division

2. Sally has 32 books. She wants to put the same number of books into each of her 8 boxes. How many books will go in each box?
- (A) addition
- (B) subtraction
- (C) multiplication
- (D) division

3. Each of the children at the party wants to eat 2 pieces of pizza. If there are 12 children, then how many pieces of pizza are needed to feed them all?
- (A) addition
- (B) subtraction
- (C) multiplication
- (D) division

4. Dominick walked 3 miles on Tuesday. On Wednesday he walked 2 miles farther than he did the day before. How many miles did Dominick walk on Wednesday?
- (A) addition
- (B) subtraction
- (C) multiplication
- (D) division

5. Cathy was 87 pounds in March. Two months later she had lost 5 pounds. How much did Cathy weigh in May?
- (A) addition
- (B) subtraction
- (C) multiplication
- (D) division

6. Jenny bought three magazines at the newsstand. If each magazine cost $3.99, how much did Jenny pay?
- (A) addition
- (B) subtraction
- (C) multiplication
- (D) division

7. Lee owns 12 pairs of shoes. She wants to buy a shoe rack that holds 24 pairs. How many more pairs of shoes can Lee fit on the shoe rack?
- (A) addition
- (B) subtraction
- (C) multiplication
- (D) division

8. Johnny has 18 toy cars. For his birthday he is getting 6 more. How many toy cars will he have after his birthday?
- (A) addition
- (B) subtraction
- (C) multiplication
- (D) division

Writing a Number Sentence

Choose the number sentence that would be used to answer the question.

1. The average honeybee makes about $\frac{1}{12}$ teaspoon of honey in its lifetime. How many bees would it take to make $\frac{1}{4}$ teaspoon of honey?

   Ⓐ $\frac{1}{12} \div \frac{1}{4} =$

   Ⓑ $\frac{1}{4} \div \frac{1}{12} =$

   Ⓒ $\frac{1}{4} \times \frac{1}{12} =$

   Ⓓ $\frac{1}{4} - \frac{1}{12} =$

2. The average chicken egg weighs 50 grams. A chicken lays an egg that is 15 grams below average. What is the weight of the egg?

   Ⓐ 50 − 15 =

   Ⓑ 50 + 15 =

   Ⓒ 50 ÷ 150=

   Ⓓ 15 − 50 =

3. A library has 8,000 books. If the books are spread out evenly between 25 shelves, then how many books are on each shelf?

   Ⓐ 8,000 − 25 =

   Ⓑ 8,000 + 25 =

   Ⓒ 25 ÷ 8,000 =

   Ⓓ 8,000 ÷ 25 =

4. There are 7 squirrels living in a tree. Each squirrel collects 12 acorns for the winter. How many acorns are there total?

   Ⓐ 12 ÷ 7 =

   Ⓑ 7 + 12 =

   Ⓒ 7 × 12 =

   Ⓓ 12 − 7 =

5. A box of doughnuts at the store costs $1.75. Tax on the doughnuts is $0.35. How much do the doughnuts cost after tax?

   Ⓐ $1.75 − $0.35 =

   Ⓑ $1.75 ÷ $0.35 =

   Ⓒ $1.75 + $0.35 =

   Ⓓ $1.75 × $0.35 =

6. A record store is offering 40% off of CDs that cost $20 or more. How much is the discount on a $20 CD?

   Ⓐ $20 − .40 =

   Ⓑ $20 × .40 =

   Ⓒ $20 ÷ 40 =

   Ⓓ $20 + 40 =

Identifying Missing Information

Answer the questions below.

1. A runner is preparing to run a marathon. It takes the runner 8 minutes to run 1 mile. What other information is needed to determine how long it will take the runner to finish the marathon?
   - Ⓐ the time the marathon starts
   - Ⓑ the age of the runner
   - Ⓒ the location of the marathon
   - Ⓓ the length of the marathon

2. Casey wants to paint his ceiling red. The ceiling has an area of 100 ft². What other information is needed to determine how much paint Casey will need?
   - Ⓐ the area that one can of paint will cover
   - Ⓑ the cost of a can of paint
   - Ⓒ the size of Casey's house
   - Ⓓ Casey's favorite color

3. Mary got a chocolate cake for her birthday party. Mary and her friends each ate 2 pieces of cake. What other information is needed to determine how many pieces of cake were eaten at the party?
   - Ⓐ the size of the cake
   - Ⓑ the size of each slice of cake
   - Ⓒ the number of friends
   - Ⓓ the age of Mary's friends

4. Jeffrey loves to read. He can read 1 page in 1 minute. What other information is needed to determine how long it will take for Jeffrey to read a book?
   - Ⓐ the number of words on each page
   - Ⓑ the weight of the book
   - Ⓒ the time of day
   - Ⓓ the number of pages in the book

5. A candle melts 1.5 inches every hour. What other information is needed to determine how long the candle is after 3 hours?
   - Ⓐ the color of the candle
   - Ⓑ the length of the candle at the start
   - Ⓒ the location of the candle
   - Ⓓ the weight of the candle

6. Jeremy buys a 20-lb bag of cat litter every two weeks. What other information is needed to determine how much money Jeremy spends on cat litter in a month?
   - Ⓐ the brand of cat litter
   - Ⓑ his cat's weight
   - Ⓒ the amount of cat litter he uses a day
   - Ⓓ the cost of a 20-lb bag of cat litter

Identifying Extra Information

For each word problem, choose the extra information that is not needed to solve the problem.

1. A certain car gets 30 miles per gallon of gas. Gas costs $3.00 per gallon and the gas tank holds 10 gallons. How far will the car go if $6.50 of gas is purchased?
Ⓐ the capacity of the gas tank
Ⓑ the cost of gas per gallon
Ⓒ the amount of miles per gallon
Ⓓ the amount of gas purchased

2. A video game starts you with 4 lives. Every coin collected gives you 1,000 points. If you get an extra life for every 100,000 points, then how many extra lives would you get if you collected 300 coins?
Ⓐ the number of points per coin
Ⓑ the number of points per extra life
Ⓒ the number of coins collected
Ⓓ the number of lives you start with

3. Danny has 42 pounds of clothes he needs to mail to a friend. Each box costs $1.00 and can hold 7 pounds. It takes Danny 3 minutes to pack each box. How long will it take Danny to pack all of the clothes?
Ⓐ the amount of clothes being sent
Ⓑ the amount of clothes each box can hold
Ⓒ the cost of each box
Ⓓ the amount of time it takes to pack a box

4. A bag of carrots costs $2.00. There are about 1,200 calories per bag. If each bag weighs one pound, how many calories will $6.00 of carrots be?
Ⓐ the cost of a bag
Ⓑ the weight of a bag
Ⓒ the number of calories per bag
Ⓓ the amount of money spent

5. A printer can print 5 pages in 1 minute. A pack of 100 pieces of paper costs $1.50. How many pieces of paper will you get for $4.50?
Ⓐ the speed of the printer
Ⓑ the cost of a pack of paper
Ⓒ the number of pieces of paper per pack
Ⓓ the amount of money spent

6. It takes Gabriela 30 minutes to get from her house to her mother's house. She is going over for dinner. At what time will she get there if she leaves at 7:35 PM?
Ⓐ where she is going
Ⓑ why she is going
Ⓒ what time she is leaving
Ⓓ how long it takes to get there

Using a Formula

Choose the formula that you would use to get the correct answer.

1. Clark wants to decorate his living room with a border around all of the walls. The length of the room is 12 feet and the width is 14 feet. How long of a border does Clark need, so that it will go all the way around the room?
   - (A) $A = 12 \times 14$
   - (B) $P = 2 \times 12 + 2 \times 14$
   - (C) $A = 2 \times 12 + 2 \times 14$
   - (D) $P = 12 \times 14$

2. Michelle wants to put all of her stuffed animals into boxes. She has boxes that are 2 feet high, 3 feet wide, and 3 feet long. How much room does each box have?
   - (A) $V = 2 \times 3 + 2 \times 3$
   - (B) $V = 3 + 3 + 2$
   - (C) $V = 3 \times 3$
   - (D) $V = 3 \times 3 \times 2$

3. An American flag at a car dealership is 2 meters long and 1.5 meters wide. How much fabric did it take to make the flag?
   - (A) $A = 2 \times 2 + 2 \times 1.5$
   - (B) $P = 2 \times 2 + 2 \times 1.5$
   - (C) $A = 2 \times 1.5$
   - (D) $P = 2 \times 2 + 2 \times 1.5$

4. Grandma makes an apple pie that is 14 inches around. What is the diameter of the pie?
   - (A) $d = \dfrac{7}{\pi}$
   - (B) $d = 14\pi$
   - (C) $d = 7\pi$
   - (D) $d = \dfrac{14}{\pi}$

5. Sandra has several fish in her fish tank. She finds out that her tank holds 54,000 cm³ of water. If the length and width of the tank are both 30 cm, then what is the height of it?
   - (A) $h = \dfrac{54,000}{30 \times 30}$
   - (B) $h = 54,000 - 30 - 30$
   - (C) $h = \dfrac{30 \times 30}{54,000}$
   - (D) $h = \dfrac{54,000 + 30}{30}$

6. If you travel on a highway at a speed of 75 mph for 7 hours and then continue for another 3 hours at a speed of 65 mph, how many miles will you have covered?
   - (A) $d = 75 \times 7 \times 65 \times 3$
   - (B) $d = 75 \times 7 + 65 \times 3$
   - (C) $d = \dfrac{75 \times 7}{65 \times 3}$
   - (D) $d = 75 \times 65 \times 10$

Solving Multi-Step Problems

Answer the questions below.

1. A plant grows 2 inches every day for the first 3 days. Every day after that it grows 1 inch. How many inches has the plant grown after 6 days?
   Ⓐ 3 in.
   Ⓑ 6 in.
   Ⓒ 9 in.
   Ⓓ 11 in.

2. Harry is selling raffle tickets for his school. The first 10 tickets are $3.00 each and every ticket after that is $2.00. How many tickets would you get for $42.00 dollars?
   Ⓐ 16
   Ⓑ 14
   Ⓒ 19
   Ⓓ 22

3. Shaquana makes $9.00 an hour at the department store she works in. On Tuesday she works 5.5 hours, and on Thursday she works 9 hours. How much money did Shaquana make for the 2 days she worked?
   Ⓐ $81.00
   Ⓑ $49.50
   Ⓒ $120.50
   Ⓓ $130.50

4. Miguel is baking desserts for his cooking class. The cookies he is making need $\frac{1}{2}$ cup sugar per batch, and the cake needs $\frac{1}{4}$ cup sugar per cake. If Miguel makes 2 cakes and 3 batches of cookies, then how much sugar does he need in all?
   Ⓐ $1\frac{3}{4}$ cups
   Ⓑ 2 cups
   Ⓒ $2\frac{1}{4}$ cups
   Ⓓ $\frac{3}{4}$ cup

5. Kaia is watching for birds in the early morning hours. Between 3 ᴀᴍ and 6 ᴀᴍ she sees about 7 birds an hour. After 6 ᴀᴍ there are only about 4 birds an hour. How many birds did Kaia see if she was bird watching from 3 ᴀᴍ to 8 ᴀᴍ?
   Ⓐ 36
   Ⓑ 29
   Ⓒ 28
   Ⓓ 24

6. Javier walks 3 miles a day Monday through Wednesday. Thursdays and Fridays he walks 4 miles a day. On weekends he walks only 2 miles a day. How many miles does he walk in a week?
   Ⓐ 168 mi
   Ⓑ 24 mi
   Ⓒ 9 mi
   Ⓓ 21 mi

Section 9: Test

Answer the questions below.

1. Which list of numbers is ordered from greatest to least?

Ⓐ $9\frac{1}{9}$, 9.9, 0.99, $\frac{1}{9}$

Ⓑ 9.9, $\frac{1}{9}$, $9\frac{1}{9}$, 0.99

Ⓒ 9.9, $9\frac{1}{9}$, 0.99, $\frac{1}{9}$

Ⓓ $9\frac{1}{9}$, 9.9, $\frac{1}{9}$, 0.99

2. The two triangles below are similar. What is the length of side y?

Ⓐ 17.5
Ⓑ 12.5
Ⓒ 24.5
Ⓓ 30

12 13
5
x 32.5
y

3. $-13 \times 9 =$

Ⓐ $\frac{9}{13}$

Ⓑ 117

Ⓒ −117

Ⓓ $-\frac{9}{13}$

4. $\frac{2}{7} + \frac{3}{11} =$

Ⓐ $\frac{5}{18}$

Ⓑ $\frac{5}{11}$

Ⓒ $\frac{47}{77}$

Ⓓ $\frac{43}{77}$

5. About how much is
1.376 − 0.547 = ?

Ⓐ 0.9
Ⓑ 0.8
Ⓒ 0.85
Ⓓ 0.88

6. If a circle has a radius of 13 cm, then what is its circumference?

Ⓐ 40.8 cm
Ⓑ 81.6 cm
Ⓒ 20.4 cm
Ⓓ 530.7 cm

7. What is the LCM of 8, 12, and 16?

Ⓐ 4
Ⓑ 8
Ⓒ 24
Ⓓ 48

8. A mother cat has a litter of 11 kittens. 3 of the kittens are black, 2 are white, and 6 are brown. What is the proportion of black kittens to total kittens?

Ⓐ $\frac{1}{2}$

Ⓑ $\frac{4}{11}$

Ⓒ $\frac{3}{11}$

Ⓓ $\frac{1}{2}$

9. $23 - 4 \times 5 + 9 =$

Ⓐ 12
Ⓑ 104
Ⓒ 228
Ⓓ −33

10. 273 is 52% of what number?

Ⓐ 525
Ⓑ 252
Ⓒ 141.96
Ⓓ 568.75

11. What is the area of the triangle below?

Ⓐ 96 cm²
Ⓑ 32 cm²
Ⓒ 84 cm²
Ⓓ 48 cm²

12 cm
8 cm

12. Solve for the variable:
$14j = 126$

Ⓐ 1,778
Ⓑ 113
Ⓒ 9
Ⓓ 0.1

13. It took a runner 18 minutes to run 2 miles. At this rate how far would the runner have run after 1.5 hours?
Ⓐ 16.67 miles
Ⓑ 13.5 miles
Ⓒ 24 miles
Ⓓ 10 miles

14. Which angle is supplementary to 74 degrees?
Ⓐ 106 degrees
Ⓑ 16 degrees
Ⓒ −74 degrees
Ⓓ −16 degrees

15. What is the rule of the following pattern?
    23, 69, 207, 621, 1,863
Ⓐ add 46
Ⓑ divide by 3
Ⓒ multiply by 3
Ⓓ add 414

16. 4 in. = _____ cm
Ⓐ 1.57
Ⓑ 6.16
Ⓒ 14.16
Ⓓ 10.16

17. Evaluate $7t - 15$ when $t = 18$.
Ⓐ 111
Ⓑ 21
Ⓒ −144
Ⓓ 2.1

18. What equation could you use to determine the radius of a circle with an area of 75 m²?
Ⓐ $75 = 2\pi r$
Ⓑ $75 = \pi + 2r$
Ⓒ $75 = \pi r^2$
Ⓓ $75 = 2\pi r^2$

19. What ordered pair would be used to represent Point A on the graph below?

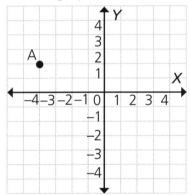

Ⓐ (2,−4)
Ⓑ (−4,2)
Ⓒ (−4,−2)
Ⓓ (−2,4)

20. Identify the type of plane figure below.

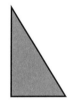

Ⓐ acute triangle
Ⓑ isosceles triangle
Ⓒ right triangle
Ⓓ obtuse triangle

21. What type of lines are shown below?

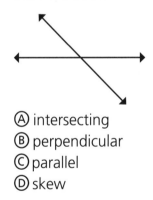

Ⓐ intersecting
Ⓑ perpendicular
Ⓒ parallel
Ⓓ skew

22. What is the probability of rolling a 6 two times in a row on a normal die?

Ⓐ $\frac{1}{6}$

Ⓑ $\frac{1}{36}$

Ⓒ $\frac{1}{35}$

Ⓓ $\frac{1}{12}$

23. Which of the following is a ray?

S   T   U

Ⓐ $\overleftarrow{TS}$

Ⓑ $\overline{SU}$

Ⓒ $\overleftrightarrow{SU}$

Ⓓ $\overleftrightarrow{TU}$

24. What unit of measure would **best** be used to see how much milk a store has?

Ⓐ pounds

Ⓑ feet

Ⓒ gallons

Ⓓ cups

25. Kayla took three tests. She scored 7, 5, and 9. After a 4th test Kayla's mean test score was 7.5. What did Kayla get on her 4th test?

Ⓐ 6

Ⓑ 7

Ⓒ 8

Ⓓ 9

26. What would be the volume of a cylinder with a diameter of 8 in. and a height of 22 in.?

Ⓐ 352 in.³

Ⓑ 1,105.3 in.³

Ⓒ 552.6 in.³

Ⓓ 4,421.1 in.³

27. What graph would **best** be used to show the change in temperature throughout the year?

Ⓐ bar graph

Ⓑ circle graph

Ⓒ line graph

Ⓓ box-and-whisker plot

28. What type of figure is shown below?

Ⓐ triangular prism

Ⓑ triangular pyramid

Ⓒ rectangular pyramid

Ⓓ rectangular prism

29. $\frac{4}{9} + \frac{7}{12} =$

Ⓐ $\frac{11}{21}$

Ⓑ $1\frac{1}{36}$

Ⓒ $1\frac{7}{9}$

Ⓓ $3\frac{1}{3}$

30. Kaleb has to dust the house for his mom. It takes Kaleb 20 minutes to dust one room. There are 7 rooms in the house. What operation would you use to determine how long it will take Kaleb to dust the whole house?

Ⓐ addition

Ⓑ subtraction

Ⓒ multiplication

Ⓓ division

31. 385 is 40% of which number?

Ⓐ 616
Ⓑ 641.67
Ⓒ 1,540
Ⓓ 962.5

32. 2 mi. = _____ ft

Ⓐ 10,760
Ⓑ 8,560
Ⓒ 10,560
Ⓓ 8,520

33. What would be the new coordinates of Point A at (2,3) if it was translated up 2 and right 3?

Ⓐ (5,5)
Ⓑ (4,6)
Ⓒ (0,0)
Ⓓ (−1,1)

34. $\frac{5}{8} + \frac{7}{9} =$

Ⓐ $1\frac{1}{6}$
Ⓑ $1\frac{29}{72}$
Ⓒ $\frac{3}{4}$
Ⓓ $\frac{45}{72}$

35. Jamal is buying party favors for his friends. Each of the party favors costs $1.50. What piece of information is needed to determine how much Jamal will have to spend to get all of his friends party favors?

Ⓐ the amount of money Jamal has
Ⓑ the age of Jamal and his friends
Ⓒ the time of the party
Ⓓ the number of friends coming to the party

36. A box has 12 colored cards inside it. 3 of the cards are blue, 2 are white, 5 are yellow, and 2 are green. What is the probability that a card drawn at random will be white or green?

Ⓐ $\frac{1}{2}$
Ⓑ $\frac{1}{4}$
Ⓒ $\frac{1}{3}$
Ⓓ $\frac{2}{3}$

37. The chart below shows how Janet spent her money last month. If her total monthly spending was $1,800, then how much was spent on gas?

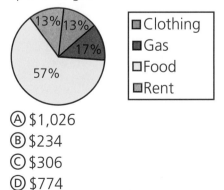

■	Clothing
■	Gas
☐	Food
■	Rent

13% 13% 17% 57%

Ⓐ $1,026
Ⓑ $234
Ⓒ $306
Ⓓ $774

38. On Monday night, 1 inch of snow fell every 2 hours until 11 PM. After 11 PM, snow fell 0.5 inches every 2 hours. How much snow fell between 9 PM and 3 AM?

Ⓐ 2 inches
Ⓑ 1.5 inches
Ⓒ 3 inches
Ⓓ 2.5 inches

Answer Key

Pages 8–9
1. C
2. D
3. C
4. A
5. D
6. B
7. C
8. B

Pages 10–11
1. B
2. B
3. C
4. C
5. A
6. A
7. C
8. D
9. D
10. B

Pages 12–13
1. B
2. D
3. C
4. B
5. D
6. A
7. C
8. D
9. C
10. D

Pages 14–15
1. C
2. D
3. B
4. C
5. B
6. B

Pages 16–17
1. C
2. A
3. B
4. C
5. D
6. B
7. D
8. C
9. D
10. C

Pages 18–19
1. B
2. B
3. D
4. A
5. D
6. C
7. D
8. B

Pages 20–21
1. A
2. B
3. B
4. C
5. D
6. C
7. A
8. B
9. D
10. C

Pages 22–23
1. C
2. D
3. B
4. A
5. C
6. C
7. B
8. D
9. A
10. A

Pages 24–25
1. B
2. A
3. C
4. B
5. D
6. A
7. C
8. B
9. D
10. B
11. A
12. D

Pages 26–27
1. B
2. D
3. C
4. B
5. A
6. D
7. C
8. A
9. C
10. D
11. A
12. A
13. B
14. D

Pages 28–29
1. B
2. C
3. B
4. D
5. C
6. D
7. D
8. C
9. A

10. A
11. C
12. B

Pages 30–31
1. B
2. B
3. D
4. A
5. D
6. B
7. A
8. C
9. A
10. D

Pages 32–33
1. D
2. B
3. A
4. D
5. B
6. C

Pages 34–35
1. D
2. B
3. D
4. C
5. A
6. B
7. A
8. B
9. A
10. A

Pages 36–37
1. A
2. A
3. D
4. B
5. C
6. A
7. D
8. D
9. D
10. A
11. C
12. C
13. A
14. C
15. A
16. D
17. C
18. D

Pages 38–39
1. B
2. D
3. A
4. A
5. D
6. A
7. C

8. A
9. C
10. C
11. D
12. B
13. A
14. B
15. A
16. D

Pages 40–41
1. D
2. A
3. B
4. A
5. C
6. A
7. A
8. C
9. A
10. A
11. D
12. B
13. C
14. D

Pages 42–43
1. D
2. B
3. C
4. C
5. D
6. B
7. B
8. A
9. D
10. C
11. A
12. C
13. C
14. D
15. A
16. B
17. C
18. A
19. C
20. A

Pages 44–45
1. A
2. A
3. B
4. C
5. D
6. C
7. B
8. D
9. B
10. B
11. B
12. C
13. B
14. D
15. C

16. D

Pages 46–49
1. C
2. B
3. B
4. A
5. A
6. C
7. B
8. D
9. A
10. B
11. D
12. C
13. B
14. A
15. B
16. D
17. C
18. A
19. D
20. C

Page 50
1. C
2. B
3. D
4. C
5. A
6. D
7. C
8. A

Page 51
1. C
2. C
3. C
4. B
5. C
6. D
7. A
8. B
9. D

Page 52
1. A
2. C
3. C
4. D
5. B
6. B
7. A
8. B
9. A
10. D
11. C
12. A

Page 53
1. B
2. B
3. A
4. C
5. D
6. A
7. B
8. C
9. A

Pages 54–55
1. B
2. C
3. C
4. A
5. D
6. A
7. B
8. D
9. D
10. B
11. B
12. C
13. D
14. A
15. C
16. B
17. A
18. D

Pages 56–57
1. C
2. D
3. C
4. B
5. A
6. C
7. A
8. D
9. B
10. D
11. C
12. A
13. A
14. D
15. C
16. A
17. B
18. C

Page 58
1. D
2. A
3. B
4. C
5. A
6. B
7. A
8. D
9. C
10. D
11. B
12. D

Page 59
1. C
2. A
3. D
4. A
5. C
6. D
7. A
8. A
9. D
10. B
11. C
12. D

Page 60
1. C
2. B
3. D
4. A
5. B
6. C
7. A
8. C

Page 61
1. C
2. D
3. C
4. A
5. B
6. B
7. D
8. D

Page 62
1. C
2. B
3. D
4. A
5. A
6. B

Page 63
1. C
2. D
3. A
4. B
5. C
6. C
7. B
8. C
9. C
10. C
11. B
12. A

Page 64
1. C
2. A
3. D
4. B
5. A
6. C
7. B
8. A
9. C
10. D

Page 65
1. A
2. B
3. D
4. B
5. C
6. D
7. B
8. C

Page 66
1. B
2. C
3. A
4. C
5. D
6. A
7. B
8. D
9. B

Page 67
1. A
2. C
3. B
4. D
5. B
6. A
7. A
8. C
9. D

Page 68
1. C
2. B
3. B
4. C
5. B
6. D
7. C
8. B
9. A

Page 69
1. B
2. D
3. A
4. D
5. A
6. A
7. C
8. C

Pages 70–71
1. C
2. C
3. A
4. D
5. D
6. A
7. D
8. C
9. B
10. A
11. B
12. C
13. B
14. C
15. D
16. A
17. B
18. C
19. B
20. A
21. C
22. D

Page 72
1. B
2. B
3. D
4. C
5. A
6. D
7. A
8. B

Page 73
1. B
2. D
3. B
4. A

5. C
6. A
7. C
8. D
9. B
10. B

Page 74
1. D
2. A
3. C
4. B
5. D
6. C
7. B
8. A

Page 75
1. B
2. C
3. C
4. D
5. A

Page 76
1. B
2. A
3. C
4. D
5. A
6. D
7. C
8. A

Page 77
1. A
2. C
3. D
4. B
5. D
6. A
7. B
8. A

Page 78
1. C
2. A
3. B
4. D
5. B
6. D

Page 79
1. C
2. A
3. B
4. A
5. C
6. C
7. B
8. D

Page 80
1. B
2. A
3. C
4. B

Page 81
1. B
2. C
3. B
4. A
5. B
6. D

Pages 82–83
1. D
2. B
3. C
4. A
5. C
6. B
7. D
8. A
9. A
10. B

Page 84
1. B
2. D
3. C
4. A
5. B
6. C
7. B
8. A

Page 85
1. B
2. A
3. D
4. C
5. C
6. B

Page 86
1. D
2. A
3. C
4. D
5. B
6. D

Page 87
1. A
2. D
3. C
4. B
5. A
6. B

Page 88
1. B
2. D
3. C
4. D
5. A
6. B

Page 89
1. C
2. A
3. D
4. B
5. B
6. D

Pages 90–93
1. C
2. B
3. C
4. D
5. A
6. B
7. D
8. C
9. A
10. A
11. D
12. C
13. D
14. A
15. C
16. D
17. A
18. C
19. B
20. C
21. A
22. B
23. A
24. C
25. D
26. B
27. C
28. A
29. B
30. C
31. D
32. C
33. A
34. B
35. D
36. C
37. C
38. A